HERITAGE BUILDERS

A NAME FORGOTTEN

A HASTY VOW
A LOST LEGACY
A FORGOTTEN HERO

....

C.T.L. SPEAR

OBSCURE CHARACTER SERIES VOLUME II

HERITAGE BUILDERS PUBLISHING
MONTEREY, CLOVIS CALIFORNIA

Should Christians make vows?
Am I too young to make a vow?
Isn't it foolish to vow?
To Vow or Not to Vow . . .
That is the Question

TO OUR GRANDCHILDREN
CHRYSTAL
KALI
ANTHONY
ABIGAIL
HAYLEY
KYLA
SOPHIA
JAXSON
RYDER

Dedicated to each with hope
that your name
will be remembered
for living out vows that honor our
LORD JESUS CHRIST

HERITAGE BUILDERS PUBLISHING
© 2015

First Edition 2015

Contributing Editor, Mason Smith
Cover Design, Carolyn LaPorte
Book Design, Nord Compo
Published by Heritage Builders Publishing
Clovis, Monterey California 93619
www.HeritageBuilders.com   1-888-898-9563

ISBN 978-1-942603-15-3

Printed and bound in United States of America

CONTENTS

ACKNOWLEDGEMENTS

Fascination with obscure Bible characters began for me during childhood. My mother quoting Scripture beside my crib is still a vivid memory reflecting back to Stegall, Nebraska, an unincorporated town of less than ten residents. I was under four years of age.

Later, the daily Family Altar time after breakfast covered varied topics in spoon-sized bites of Scripture, a devotional reading, a snippet of poetry, and a summary quote from Our Daily Bread, a publication of Radio Bible Class, Grand Rapids, Michigan.

A steady flow of pastors, evangelists, and missionaries appeared at area churches, youth rallies, and at Maranatha Bible Camp, where I vowed to devote my life to Christian service at age eleven. The influence of godly Sunday school teachers instilled curiosity and fired my imagination with the exploits of Bible heroes, missionaries, and evangelists.

As a twenty-year-old church planter and Bible College student, I had so little to offer as a preacher. What else could be said about David and Goliath? Peter walking on water? Samson or Noah? I began exploring inconspicuous Bible personalities like Jephthah, Shammah, and Benaiah.

One Sunday school teacher made Old Testament stories live for a fourth grade boy who never forgot, and grew up to preach them. Thank God for the faithful prayers and diligent teaching of Mrs. Shirley Scott at the Berean Church in Scottsbluff, Nebraska.

A significant amount of editorial assistance and counsel about cover design was provided by the author's wife, Sharen, and his daughters, Dayna Guenther, and Kendra Carter, and daughter-in-love, Erin Love Spear.

Author's advisory

The author has taken the liberty to use boldface for emphasis, and all scripture citations are printed in italic from the King James Version. Some segments, especially toward the end of the book, are fictionalized for the purpose of illustrating the author's interpretation and application of the hero's story.

THE FATEFUL VOW

"Now Jephthah the Gileadite was a mighty man of valour, and he was the son of an harlot: and Gilead begat Jephthah.

2. And Gilead's wife bare him sons; and his wife's sons grew up, and they thrust out Jephthah, and said unto him, Thou shalt not inherit in our father's house; for thou art the son of a strange woman.

3. Then Jephthah fled from his brethren, and dwelt in the land of Tob: and there were gathered vain men to Jephthah, and went out with him.

4. And it came to pass in process of time, that the children of Ammon made war against Israel.

5. And it was so, that when the children of Ammon made war against Israel, the elders of Gilead went to fetch Jephthah out of the land of Tob:

6. And they said unto Jephthah, Come, and be our captain, that we may fight with the children of Ammon.

7. And Jephthah said unto the elders of Gilead, Did not ye hate me, and expel me out of my father's house? and why are ye come unto me now when ye are in distress?

8. And the elders of Gilead said unto Jephthah, Therefore we turn again to thee now, that thou mayest go with us, and fight against the children of Ammon, and be our head over all the inhabitants of Gilead.

9. And Jephthah said unto the elders of Gilead, If ye bring me home again to fight against the children of Ammon, and the Lord deliver them before me, shall I be your head?

10. And the elders of Gilead said unto Jephthah, The Lord be witness between us, if we do not so according to thy words.

11. Then Jephthah went with the elders of Gilead, and the people made him head and captain over them: and Jephthah uttered all his words before the Lord in Mizpeh.

29. Then the Spirit of the Lord came upon Jephthah, and he passed over Gilead, and Manasseh, and passed over Mizpeh of Gilead, and from Mizpeh of Gilead he passed over unto the children of Ammon.

30. And Jephthah vowed a vow unto the Lord, and said, If thou shalt without fail deliver the children of Ammon into mine hands,

31. Then it shall be, that whatsoever cometh forth of the doors of my house to meet me, when I return in peace from the children of Ammon, shall surely be the Lord's, and I will offer it up for a burnt offering."

Judges 11: 1-11, 29-31

"Your story is the greatest legacy that you will leave to your friends. It's the longest lasting legacy you will leave to your heirs."

—Steve Saint[1]

....

1

A NAME TO REMEMBER

He left home at the age of fifteen, devoting everything to his drug addiction and the lucrative income generated by cruel management of the drug trade that was a growth industry in his hometown.

Although he was tall, he was also unusually slender, causing strangers to underestimate his volatile, sudden wrath, his calculating, brilliant mind, and the influence he wielded among his peers. As a lad, he retained control of television channel selection by holding his older sisters at bay with a BB gun. He proved his tyranny by various means, including shooting Darlene in the leg with a dart.

Resourceful in battle, he once pulled off his cowboy boot in a school classroom and waited until his enemy walked unsuspectingly down the aisle between the desks. Leaping into action, he gripped the boot with two fingers through its calf loops, and mercilessly rained down torments upon his adversary's head, face and body.

FOURTEEN FELONIES

He worked both sides of the street as a narc, infiltrating drug-pushing operations, reporting to the police, watching the arrests from a distance, and then taking over drug operations to reap greater financial income. But, at age nineteen, he was facing fourteen felonies with sentencing guidelines dictating twenty-five to seventy-five years in the New Mexico State Penitentiary.

Long before this, he was completely disowned by his father, who refused to associate with him or even publicly acknowledge him as his child. His maternal grandfather paid his bail and asked where he wanted to go.

He said, "Take me to my sister's house." Norma, his sister, allowed him to stay at her home until the arraignment. She asked a local Baptist pastor to visit him.

Pastor Doyel was very direct, confronting Steve Ragland[2] with his sin against God, Divine wrath against sin, the ultimate wages of sin in Hellfire, and the love of God revealed in the substitutionary sacrifice made willingly by the Lord Jesus Christ on the cross of Calvary. Holy Spirit conviction enveloped the young criminal's soul, and he cried out to the resurrected Christ for mercy and grace.

After the pastor left, Steve pondered the eternal implications of his newfound salvation, and stepped outside into the arid breeze of Tucumcari, New Mexico. Energized with amazement at God's love, he ran around the city block, shouting, "I'm saved! I'm saved!"

A GODLESS CHILDHOOD

As the court hearing approached, he read the Bible, prayed and listened to the counsel of the pastor. He had never attended Sunday school or church, because his parents were backslidden believers, and his dad did not want to hear anything about God in their home. Although his parents had been saved during their teenage years, they did not go to church and fell into a life of drinking and partying. Their children grew up completely godless, but the Lord in mercy answered a grandmother's prayers. After

Steve was saved, his mom and dad recognized the goodness of God and rededicated their lives to the Lord.

HIS VOW TO GOD

As Steve reflected on God's forgiveness, he was impressed with the power of God. Instructed in the basics of prayer, he made a vow to God to tell the truth in court, answering honestly, but not volunteering information.

After the prosecution presented its case, cross-examination began. Years later, Bud Ragland, Steve's dad commented, "I don't know if that boy ever told the truth about anything before he was saved!"

Somehow, he answered truthfully in court. When all arguments had been heard, the Judge ordered him to stand for sentencing. He lifted the gavel and paused for several moments. He frowned, and said, "I don't know why I'm doing this… NINETY DAYS in the County Jail!"

During the ninety days, Steve read Scripture aloud to all the inmates every day. They read many passages, and through the book of Genesis aloud 29 times.

He painted a flatbed truck red, white and blue and parked alongside the city park in Tucumcari. He and others preached the gospel to people in the park. Many of his drug culture friends trusted Christ. He went to Bible college and married Margaret after her conversion. They served churches in New Mexico, Texas, Washington, Wyoming, and Colorado. His parents, sisters, and many family members continue serving the Lord to this day.

FOURTEEN YEARS LATER

About fourteen years after his conversion, the author met Steve Ragland in Wyoming. A few months later, he and Margaret joined our church staff, serving with us there and in Colorado, a total of four years. By that time, the governor of New Mexico had granted a full pardon for his crimes. Later, he served pastorates, earned Bachelor's, Master's and Doctoral degrees, and was a full time prison chaplain in South Dakota, working in both Federal and State penitentiaries.

Nearly thirty years after we met, I attended Steve Ragland's funeral in Tucumcari. Pastors Wes Stewart and Joe Doyel officiated and Steve and Margaret's son, Scott, a miracle child, preached Steve's funeral.

After fifteen years of marriage, Steve and Margaret had given up hope of bearing a child, but in answer to a special prayer meeting, Scott was born, the only child to carry on the family name.

A NAME TO REMEMBER

Steve Ragland's name was sure to be remembered in disgrace until the saving grace of the Lord Jesus Christ reached into his broken life. More than receiving pardon from the governor, his memory was transformed from delinquency to an honorable legacy because of the remarkable transformation of his life, a vow kept, and the influence of his testimony.

A person's name and thus, his legacy, is often tainted by or redeemed by one decision. A single choice for good may be the one thing for which we are remembered. There are many examples in history. Benedict Arnold's name might not have become a synonym for treachery, except for one decision to betray his country. Pinocchio's name is linked to lying. William Booth founded the Salvation Army. His life is captioned by a single word, which appears on his tombstone: Others.

Except for his decision to trust Christ as Savior, Steve Ragland's watershed choice was made the day he decided to risk everything by vowing to tell the truth in court. If he had broken that vow, the rest of his life would have been lived behind bars, and his name forgotten except to a few. By choosing eternal values, he chose an eternal legacy.

"No legacy is so rich as honesty."

—William Shakespeare[3]

2

MOTIVES FOR MAKING VOWS

A vow to God is much more than a mere human promise. It is rooted in the motives of one's heart, where intentions, thoughts, and counsels (I Corinthians 3:20-21, 4: 5, Hebrews 4: 12) are discerned. Many a lawbreaker has attempted to bargain with God, but it is pointless without Holy Spirit transformation, purifying his motives.

MORE THAN SETTING A GOAL

Because we are human we cannot foresee the pitfalls, adversity, and opposition that may be brought to bear against goals we set. There is a difference between setting a goal and making a vow. It is no child's play to make a vow.

A proper vow to God assumes that the vow-maker has taken into account that it is foolish to attempt anything without Divine approval. This is why Jesus taught us to pray "Thy will be done." (Matthew 6: 10) Plans that ignore the will of God are ill conceived at best, and arrogant at worst.

DREAM THE DREAM

Humanism coaches us to "dream the dream," but scripture teaches us to analyze facts as well as to step out by faith. That is not to say there is no place for spontaneous faith. David's mighty man, Shammah, exhibited impulsive faith when, without advance warning he trusted the Lord for an impossible victory, when under attack by the Philistines in a field of lentils (II Samuel 23: 11-12).

GOD LEADS HIS CHILDREN

Jesus didn't expect Peter to walk on water the first day they met. But, He did command him, "Follow me" (Matthew 4: 19). God leads his dear children along from one step of faith to the next. Baby steps include infant vows. The famous industrialist, R.G. LeTourneau began by promising to give ten percent of his income to the Lord. As his faith grew, he eventually gave ninety percent and lived on ten.

There is usually a space of time between the making of a vow and its fulfillment. Thirty-two thousand men volunteered to help Gideon attack the Midianites, but he ended up with only three hundred (Judges 7: 1-8). It took the stability of integrity in those three hundred to see it through.

AN OBSCURE PERSON

A most unlikely Bible personality, Jephthah, is the hero of this book. Integrity cost him far more than he expected. In many ways, his story is a detour in the history of his time. The only passage giving his story (Judges 11: 1- 12: 7) is a parenthesis in some ways. A mere record of the history would not require the amount of detail given. There must be a larger reason why his tale is told.

His vow seems to have been his undoing. Rejected by his family, he returned to become the hero in a war that saved his clan and kept the enemy from invading the entire Israeli nation. It is an epic story of a major triumph.

If only the story could have ended there, it would have been far less stressful for the major characters of the drama. But, if it had, it would be just another story about a local boy who made good. It is an interesting plot, but not exactly one we've never heard before.

THE VICTORY PARADE DISASTER

At the ultimate crescendo of his triumphant victory march and return to his own home, the whole scene descended into the pits, when his daughter pranced out, cheering his greatest moment, but not realizing that he had vowed to sacrifice to God "whatsoever" came to meet him upon his return. His words convey the awful rending of his heart, "Alas, my daughter! thou hast brought me very low, and thou art one of them that trouble me: for I have opened my mouth unto the Lord, and I cannot go back." (Judges 11: 35)

Was Jephthah's vow just a hasty, foolish edict, like that of the inebriated King Herod, who took an oath to give Salome,[4] the dancer, whatever she asked? (Matthew 14: 7)

Was it as impetuous as Ahasuerus' accommodation to murderous Haman's request for authority to annihilate the Jews? (Esther 3: 10-13)

Was it as ill advised as the decree of Darius, which condemned Daniel to the lion's den? (Daniel 6: 6-9)

Many have summarily judged Jephthah and dismissed him to obscurity. His is a name forgotten, even to many serious Bible students. What if he had never made his controversial vow?

"I don't know how an oath becomes meaningful unless you have faith. Because at the end you say, 'So help me God.' And a promise to God is different from a promise to anyone else."

—Justice Clarence Thomas[5]
United States Supreme Court

3

THE VALUE OF A VOW

My sweetheart and I faced the pastor surrounded by our witnesses and a leafy hedge, cleverly improvised by stapling newly harvested branches of shrubbery to green painted plywood bordering the church platform. A fountain powered by an electric motor gurgled nearby. My fiancé was the only daughter of a prosperous Minnesota farmer. No expense had been spared for the June wedding.

Her mother had battled cancer for several years, making frequent trips to Mayo clinic in Rochester, 130 miles away. The eventual death sentence had been pronounced when she was forty, refocusing her life on immediate goals of seeing her first grandchild, her children's graduations and her daughter's wedding. For seventeen torturous years, she achieved temporal goals one by one, only to press on unrelentingly toward another.

VOWS SET TO MUSIC

The bride's college friend played the organ prelude masterfully. She accompanied the bride's brother, who sang the song of King David's grandmother, "Entreat Me Not to Leave Thee." Instead of the usual "Here Comes the Bride," she played the introduction to "O Promise Me," for which we wrote and substituted a new verse. The groom sang:

"O promise me today that you and I
Will consecrate our selves to God on high.
We'll serve our Saviour now; our whole lives through
As one, we now declare we will be true.
Our home will be a place where God is first,
For, only He can quench an inner thirst.
To serve our God, our one desire will be.
O promise me, O promise me.[6]

It was a traditional ceremony. The vows were phrases often eliminated as too restrictive in these progressive days of the twenty-first century.

TRADITIONAL VOWS

Is there really any value to the making of a vow? In today's world, marriage vows are broken with such frequency that traditional vows once used in wedding ceremonies have almost disappeared.

Colonial America was a society in which "a man's word was his bond." A handshake was as good as a contract. Men valued their commitments because their reputation was at stake.

Modern youth has little appreciation for the strength of vows made by their ancestors. Those who have grown up on cartoons and online video games might only view a vow to kill as one to be taken seriously.

AT THE ALTAR

Marriage vows made before God and witnesses were honored in North America a century or two ago, and other vows of consecration made by Christian workers were not taken lightly. This was the climate in which men of God gave altar calls and invitations. Evangelist Charles Finney taught preachers to "preach to a verdict." A lawyer converted from a skeptical view of God and the Bible, Finney is often credited with introducing the practice that some refer to as "the modern invitational system." He urged listeners to renounce the past, take an open stand, and embrace Christ in a public venue.

A RELIC OF THE PAST

Today, many see the altar call as a relic of the past. Pastors trained by professional theologians are given little positive reinforcement or instruction about invitations. Bible Colleges and seminaries value advanced academic credentials over evangelistic experience. In a seminary library, the author reviewed a Master's degree thesis on "The Modern Invitational System," which claimed there is no scriptural basis for its use.

Is it wrong to compel a decision? Was something essential lost in abandoning the altar call? No doubt, some have allowed the invitation to become a ritual without passion. Some view it as merely a part of the culture of certain denominations or regions of the country.

For some, the altar call is only a tradition. It is a feature of the program in which the faithful are expected to file dutifully to the platform area, and kneel in an attitude of prayer. The spirit of this part of the meeting reveals inner motivations both of leadership and those who respond.

Others dismiss the practice citing lack of support from history or scripture. The author sees I Corinthians 14:24-25 as a key passage intimating an "altar call" type of response in the apostolic era.

A SPIRITUAL VOW

In 1899, Lincoln McConnell, southern preacher and popular Chautauqua comedian, brought his tent from Georgia to towns along the Oregon Trail. He preached many weeks, attracting residents and covered wagon travelers.

My great grandparents, Clarence and Sarah Spear had lived a decade in Clay County, Nebraska, preparing for the trek west to homestead territory in the state's panhandle. On the last night of the evangelistic campaign, their stubborn Irish pride finally surrendered. Publicly, they walked the aisle together, confessing their personal faith in Christ, a vow not taken lightly.

Their youngest son, my granddad, was ten, but he never forgot that momentous hour. Although he did not personally trust Christ as Savior for another thirty-two years, he remembered it in vivid detail sixty-five years later as with great emotion he recounted the event to me.

CHARACTER MAKES THE DIFFERENCE

It was not the altar call, nor yet the passion of the preacher that made a lifelong impression. The character of the couple making their way to the altar was typical for pioneers of that era. They would no more have responded to the invitation with a flippant attitude or just to see what it was about than they would have brandished a pistol to rob the offering. Their inner conviction was that the message, the messenger, and the meeting were holy in nature, presenting an opportunity to be truly converted.

Those void of character think nothing of making vows to God on Sunday morning and breaking them before mid- afternoon. These are people who regularly evade paying debts, glibly choose bankruptcy, ignore promises, and refuse responsibility for their own children.

Spiritual awakenings of the past, whether personal, congregational, or national, were undergirded by prayer habits of people whose character had been transformed.

The disciples met for heart-searching prayer many days before the Day of Pentecost came. They had learned how vital prayer was at Gethsemane.

The Biblical principle, "If my people... shall humble themselves, and pray, and seek my face, and turn from their wicked ways;" (II Chronicles 7: 14) was connected to specific historical events, but James makes it clear that "The effectual fervent prayer of a righteous man availeth much." He illustrated using the effective prayer of "Elias... a man subject to like passions as we are," who prayed earnestly that rain would cease. It dried up for three years, which got everyone's attention. And, it didn't rain again until he prayed, requesting it (James 5: 16-18, I Kings 17-18).

We live among spiritually careless people. Not just the ungodly, but believers are also apathetic. In such an environment, every individual must answer for himself: to vow or not to vow— that is the question that focuses like a laser on the integrity or lack thereof, which makes one's name noteworthy or forgettable.

"Be sure you're right. Then go ahead."

—Davy Crockett [7]

....

4

THE COST OF INTEGRITY

Israel's King David described a life of stability in a song, which might properly be called the Psalm of Integrity. One feature of David's description of integrity reads, "He that sweareth to his own hurt, and changeth not." (Psalm 15: 4) David taught that the Lord puts a premium on the kind of character that makes a promise and keeps it. The commitment may turn out to hurt the person who made it, but he still stands by it, because of his integrity.

Integrity is a trait that must be developed. It is not inherited; not passed on genetically nor part of one's natural temperament. Even those who get a poor start in life can still develop integrity. Most of this book is focused on an obscure fellow, Jephthah, who through no fault of his own, got a bad start in life. Although forgotten by most Bible readers, God put the spotlight on him in a very special way, apparently because of his integrity. He has been faulted for the vow he made, yet it seems that vow was the very thing that placed him in God's showcase, making his name memorable.

INTEGRITY: HONESTY, ETHICS

A simple definition of integrity is "honesty," used in the sense of being what we appear to be. This is more than just telling the truth. Living the truth inside and out, integrity adheres to moral and ethical principles. It is often used to describe the state of being whole or complete, as in "the integrity of a ship's hull."[8]

God asked Satan, "Hast thou considered my servant Job, that there is none like him in the earth, a perfect and an upright man, one that feareth God, and escheweth evil? and still he holdeth fast his integrity, although thou movest me against him, to destroy him without cause." (Job 2: 3)

Later, Job's wife asked her beleaguered husband, "Dost thou still retain thine integrity?" (Job 2: 9)

WILLIAM CAREY'S VOW

William Carey is recognized as the Father of Modern Missions. A shoe cobbler by trade, surrounded by Baptists who subscribed to an extreme Calvinistic view of Scripture, Carey nonetheless became convinced that it is the duty and calling of believers to take the gospel of Jesus Christ to the entire world. While repairing shoes, he taught himself Latin, Greek, Hebrew, Italian, Dutch, and French as well as the Bible.

Challenging the status quo, he aroused the interest and support of Baptist churches in England, organized a mission agency, and sailed for India. However, he soon had to obtain secular work for a livelihood because funding from England evaporated. Supporters, who had never seen his mission field, withdrew their support. He could have gone home in defeat, but retaining his integrity, he found a job and continued his missionary work for a lifetime.

Another missionary, Dr. John Thomas a physician closely associated with Carey in India, was a poor money manager who repeatedly overextended his accounts. More than once, Carey's integrity bailed his friend out of debt in order to protect the testimony of their work.

PROBLEMS AT HOME

Carey's wife never adjusted to living in India. Unable to cope, she became mentally ill and even attacked him with a knife. Both his wife and child died. Still, he clung to his vow to remain a missionary to the people of India.

Working secular jobs, battling the emotional stresses of a difficult marriage, and paying off Dr. Thomas's debts, he labored to win souls and establish churches. In the process, he printed scripture in 44 languages and dialects and was appointed Professor of Bengali at Ft. William College, where he served 30 years.[9]

He "swore to his own hurt" when he vowed to become a missionary to India. But, his missionary vision inspired a hundred years of missionary enterprise unequalled since the days of the Apostles.

Such integrity is the work of God the Holy Spirit in the heart of a yielded vessel. It insistently brings us back to the choice: to vow or not to vow—that is the question. Carey's name lives on because of the integrity that keeps its vows.

JEPHTHAH'S INTEGRITY

Jephthah is an obscure Bible character whose name is virtually forgotten in the history of mankind. Even those who remember are in conflict about particular facts and the significance of his story. We hope to show that the quality and stability of his integrity is the real reason Jephthah's biography and his name has been preserved.

"Sometimes, what looks like the best choice leads down a blind alley or a dead end street."

··

JEPHTHAH'S UNUSUAL TALE

Events of the book of Judges cover about 400 years. The entire period of the Judges' leadership, including the time of Eli and Samuel (recorded in I Samuel), is reported by Luke in the New Testament to be 450 years (Acts 13: 20). Much more could have been included in the narrative. Many other personalities lived during that 400 years, but their names are forever lost to Earth's record of human history. But God, the Editor-in-Chief, decided that Jephthah's tale should be told. His controversial vow is surely the reason.

For centuries, Bible scholars have debated the vow that Jephthah made. Should he have made this promise? The New Scofield Reference Bible captions this story, Jephthah's Rash Vow,[10] implying that he was foolish to make such an irreversible, ill-advised promise. Was he? Is this a rash vow? The implication of the Scofield footnote and of many Bible commentaries seems to be that Jephthah would have been better off not to have made the promise to sacrifice "whatsoever cometh forth of the doors of my house to meet me, when I return in peace…" (Judges 11:31)

Is that the final analysis of Jephthah's vow? Is this the precept God intended, that we must be very careful, even reluctant to make a vow to God? What view of God does that interpretation teach?

THREE CRUCIAL FACTORS

A much greater lesson in this story is that God highly values integrity in our lives. But first, let us consider three crucial factors involved in Jephthah's vow.

These factors affect each of our vows today. In fact, they determine whether we fulfill the will of God in our lives. Your decisions about the vows you are contemplating have eternal implications.

A. TRAGIC CIRCUMSTANCES

In some ways, we all face tragic circumstances. There may be people who would love to exchange with you, but that is because none of us can see all the internal biases and mechanisms at work in the lives of others. Even people who grow up in the same environment are wired differently, receive unequal treatment from family and friends, and end up seeing events and ideas from opposite perspectives. It is too easy to assume a Monday morning quarterback stance when we glance down from the stadium of life, making cursory, unfair and impetuous assessments of the things others have to deal with.

B. TRAUMATIC CRISES

Accidents happen. Economic realities barge into well- laid plans. Unexpected illness, bad weather, and death strikes, leaving Mr. Job penniless, childless, homeless, and friendless. Yes, even Job, the wealthiest, healthiest, friendliest, most prosperous good guy on earth faced traumatic crises. We all admire people who rise above the trauma like Joni Eareckson Tada, whose diving accident in 1967 left her a quadriplegic in a wheelchair.[11] What an amazing life and ministry she has led! But it is too easy to assume that nothing like that will ever happen to me. Jephthah probably never expected to be forced out of his own family after his father's death.

He never anticipated that his daughter would be the first one to meet him at the gate when he returned from battle. After all, he was on a roll. Things were looking up like never before. Even though life had given him many reasons to be a pessimist, he did not expect this crisis. Hear his anguish: "Alas, my daughter! thou hast brought me very low, and thou art one of them that trouble me: for I have opened my mouth unto the Lord, and I cannot go back." (Judges 11:35)

C. TRANSFORMING CHOICES

We all choose. Decisions are thought out with our best deductive reasoning, but sometimes what looks like the best choice leads down blind alleys or dead end streets. How can we anticipate which alternatives are the transforming choices? Sometimes, we don't see them coming. That is the way events developed for Jephthah. He was a brother rejected who was destined to become a name forgotten.

"A boo is a lot louder than a cheer"

—Lance Armstrong[12]

....

6

REJECTION

Nebraska's Scotts Bluff County borders Wyoming on the west. Most of my childhood took place there. But, one year, we lived in Cheyenne, Wyoming, where as a baby-boomer, I helped overpopulate Kindergarten and was therefore moved to First Grade after two weeks. Instead of learning essential Kindergarten lessons, I found myself, an over- protected firstborn, struggling to fit in socially and academically.

Back in Nebraska, I started Second Grade at the country school with eight grades in two classrooms. The boys played a form of softball called Workup, but I knew nothing about the game. I wondered why two fellows kept tossing the ball back and forth (the pitcher and catcher). One kid invited me to play. Somebody tossed me an old ball glove with no padding. One started yelling, calling me Dummy because I didn't know how to use the glove.

RELEGATED TO THE OUTFIELD

Several hollered that I was holding up the game; that I needed to "get out in the field," referring to the outfield, where you begin the rotation process to gradually work up each time a batter is "out." After the outfield positions, you advance to Shortstop, then to Third, Second, and First base, Pitcher, Catcher, and finally, Batter. Extra players were relegated to the outfield to work their way up.

"Get out in the field," made sense. The ball diamond was situated next to a cornfield behind third base. I headed for the cornfield, wanting to prove I could "do it right."

They all began yelling again, calling me names, and pointing toward the county road which served as the outfield of the ball diamond. It didn't look at all like "the field" to me. I complied, and stood where I was told, still wondering why all these angry guys would let two guys have all the fun, tossing the ball back and forth. The batters were swinging wildly, and I wondered why so few got to use those clubs. It looked like a lot more fun than standing around "in the field."

A LINE DRIVE

About that time, a batter hit a line drive, which sped directly toward my head. I hit the grit. The yelling started again with a vengeance! The batter ran the bases while the ball soared over the county road into another cornfield.

I had facilitated a home run. Nobody could advance to a better position, and it was my fault! Some were yelling that I was "worse than Leland"[13] (another athletic underachiever). Later, I learned he was the one who was often picked-on. He didn't miss the implication either. Next recess, he approached and put his fist up against my nose. It wasn't an invitation to be best friends. There was no fight that day. But, it was Rejection 101.

JEPHTHAH'S TRAGIC BEGINNING

My rejection was a piece of cake compared to Jephthah's. The first three verses of Judges 11 explain: His Dad, Gilead, got involved with a prostitute, who gave birth to Jephthah. The Bible spares the details, but Gilead brought the boy home to grow up among his other children.

The Bible does not specify whether this took place before Gilead married, or afterward, and whether Jephthah was the firstborn, or a younger sibling. Either way, we can imagine the stress this brought to Gilead's marriage and the rejection the boy might have experienced from his stepmother. His brothers made it clear that they wouldn't share the inheritance and ran him out of the country.

THE NO-SPIN ZONE

The Bible doesn't whitewash Jephthah's actions. It tells us "there were gathered vain men to Jephthah, and went out with him." (Judges 11: 3) He threw caution and Jewish training to the wind and lived a riotous life, possibly even taking the wrong side of the law, as a leader of lawbreakers.

His exploits became so widely known that his "tough guy" persona was reported back in his hometown. When his brothers became desperate for an enforcer, their number one candidate was the brother they had rejected.

Perhaps, like Joseph's older brothers (Genesis 37), they had ganged up on him for years and knew first-hand how resourceful he could be in a fight.

EASY-GOING?

It is possible that, up until the inheritance crisis, Jephthah was an easy-going sort, who didn't anticipate his brothers' opposition. It seems that he complied with their demands with little resistance, whether out of the pain of personal rejection, or the strength of their unified intimidation. There is reason to doubt that Jephthah had been much of a threat to the brothers before their rejection. It may be that they were surprised to learn of Jephthah's adventures as a desperado. Some people's temperament comes with a long fuse. His anger may not have reached full strength until he was far away in Tob.

HIS FIGHTING SIDE

On the other hand, they may never have seen the fighting side of Jephthah. But now, when they learned of his success in battle, coupled with the imminent threat of attack on the home front, they considered that they had been too hasty, and that eating humble pie would be better than major losses and death. And, if Gilead, their father, did rear them in a god-fearing home during their formative years, perhaps they now regretted their greed, remembering Jephthah's tenacity and fierce loyalty to principle.

Every family has its own set of dynamic factors. The Bible gives us glimpses of the pressures affecting Jephthah, but it leaves room for a variety of alternative applications to our own experience.

FAMILY DYNAMICS

Jephthah's situation is not difficult for most of us to comprehend. We are surrounded by similar stories. Most kids today are growing up in homes with one or more adopted parent, due to the prevalence of divorce, remarriage, and multiple partners. The child's plight is often lost in larger battles.

As a Christian school administrator, I investigated and discovered that with less than 100 students, thirty-nine percent lived with one or more non-biological parent, due to adoption or a blended family. Speaking to Bible camps and youth conferences for twenty years, I heard many sad stories. Most came from Christian families trying to do it right, not from deviant or addiction-ridden homes. Still, many children and teens grow up with a lot of rejection.

Your circumstances may not be as disastrous as others, but when you are the kid, it is the only world you know. This can set you on a course compounding with complications. Selfish parents absorbed in their own emotions, fail to realize how crucial their influence is.

A GODLY STEP MOTHER?

The amazing part of Jephthah's story is that in spite of the tragic circumstances of his childhood home, he trusted the God Who redeems people who appear to be a lost cause.

The Bible leaves room to speculate. Was Jephthah's stepmother a godly woman whose burden for the plight of the boy, made her show great compassion? In spite of her own pain, caused by the betrayal of her husband, did she decide to show compassion to the boy? Did she, like Leah, (Genesis 29-30) devote herself more and more to the Lord and leave a holy impression on the lad that compelled him back from the land of Tob (Judges 11: 3-9), similar to the prodigal of Jesus' story? (Luke 15:11-32)

WAS DAD SINGLE?

It is possible that Gilead's involvement with the harlot took place before his marriage. Perhaps Jephthah was the son of a single parent, his Dad, who then married a woman, who came into the home recognizing the boy's innocence, and with full cognizance of the difficulty ahead, accepted her mission as a calling from God?

Abraham Lincoln's stepmother, Sarah, played a vital role in the budding president's development, by affirming his interest in reading and encouraging his intellectual development, which his father did not fully appreciate.[14]

A REPENTANT DAD?

If Gilead ventured into the liaison with the harlot after he had a wife and children at home, bringing the child home was risky, sure to threaten domestic tranquility. An overwhelming sense of responsibility must have driven him to do that for the sake of the child. Maybe Gilead truly repented of his sin with the harlot, and spent the rest of his life trying to right the wrongs and deal with consequences.

Godliness in the home seems to have influenced Jephthah's thinking, even while he was far from home and family, never expecting to return.

FAMILY REJECTION

Jephthah's rejection mirrors mankind's sinfulness. Nearly every home experiences some sibling rivalry or conflict, especially if inheritance is involved. "For the love of money is the root of all evil" (I Timothy 6:10). Gilead's children were not exempt.

SIBLING CONFLICT

One of the most tragic accusations leveled against Christian families is the poor testimony of quarreling adult siblings, who purport to be living for Christ.

A Christian farmer told of continuing conflict over an inheritance between Christian brothers and sisters, all successful adults, but still grievously controlled by sibling rivalry. Their testimony to ungodly neighbors, who had observed their church attendance and insistence on Bible principles in the community, was damaged because they refused to make peace among themselves.

PEACEMAKERS GET BITTER TOO

The Apostle Paul asked, "why do you not rather suffer yourselves to be defrauded?" (I Corinthians 6: 7) Maybe that is what Jephthah attempted to do when forced to leave home or continue fighting his brothers. But, later, embittered over their unjust treatment, he fell into the temptation of the shameful practices of his heathen companions in Tob.

THE TEXT IS SILENT

The Bible says nothing of conflict between Jephthah and his father, or of conflict with his stepmother. Only the attitude of his siblings, his half brothers, is clearly stated. Gilead, Jephthah's father, a grandson of Joseph's son Manasseh, was named for the Gilead region east of Jordan (like a Texan named Tex), which was given to half the tribe of Manasseh when the tribes received their inheritance. God had honored and blessed this man, making him one of the prominent landholders in Israel. Maybe this blessing was the result of his wholehearted repentance from his excursion into the world of illicit sex?

THE GODLINESS FACTOR

In any event, Gilead's son, Jephthah, though he took a prodigal detour into the land of Tob (in Syria, northeast of the region of Gilead)[15] was invited back to defend his brothers, their families, and their properties from Ammonites who threatened to oppress and subjugate them.

But, Jephthah apparently had a great deal of respect for the things of the Lord in his heart, because when contacted about coming home, his first response had to do with his faith in God (Judges 11: 9). This seems out of character, unless there is a godliness factor from childhood that is not mentioned in the story.

THE HUMAN FAMILY

The rejection of Jephthah brings to mind Isaiah's comment concerning the Messiah: "He is despised and rejected of men: a man of sorrows, and acquainted with grief: and we hid as it were our faces from him; he was despised, and we esteemed him not." (Isaiah 53: 3)

Selfishness caused the brothers to reject Jephthah. Just so, our self-centered pride rejects the Lord Jesus. Mary's other sons rejected her son Jesus until after His resurrection. John says of Jesus, "He came unto his own, and his own received him not." (John 1:11, 7: 5, Acts 1: 14)

Jephthah's brothers only got desperate enough to invite him to return when he was their only hope of deliverance. Only when our sin arouses the terror of judgment do we repent and cling to the Savior. He alone brings the deliverance of salvation.

YOUR PLIGHT

Jephthah risked everything to save his brothers from the Ammonites. Whatever property and assets Jephthah had accumulated during his exile, he sacrificed to rescue his family, although they had totally rejected him. He selflessly provided undeserved deliverance from certain slaughter.

It should be noted that the Ammonite threat had not suddenly appeared on the horizon. They were avowed enemies of Israel, especially of the two and a half tribes east of Jordan located near the Ammonite border.

The history of Israel under the Judges, is a story of spiritual warfare. The Ammonite incursion and Jephthah's response provide a parallel to every believer's need to be alert, ever ready for spiritual battle by maintaining unity with each other.

THE DELIVERER

Jephthah provides a shadow image of the Lord Jesus, the suffering Messiah prophesied by Isaiah in the same passage: "Surely he hath borne our griefs, and carried our sorrows… he was wounded for our transgressions, he was bruised for our iniquities: the chastisement of our peace was upon him…" (Isaiah 53: 4-5) The family of Gilead arrogantly rejected their brother and thrust him out, but when they faced dire straits, they pled for his assistance; indeed, for his leadership. They promised to yield leadership of the entire clan over to him, if he would return to their aid.

Like the sons of Gilead, we have rejected Christ, but He, like Jephthah, is still ready to save us! Though you have strayed from Him and denied him, he longs to fight for you and gather you into his loving arms. Instead of rejecting us, "he hath made us accepted in the beloved." (Ephesians 1: 6)

He says, "Come unto me all ye that labour and are heavy laden, and I will give you rest." (Matthew 11:28) For those who have been saved, but have gone their wanton way, there is still a way back to the place of blessing: "If we confess our sins, he is faithful and just to forgive us our sins, and to cleanse us from all unrighteousness." (I John 1: 9)

When your crisis comes, are you on speaking terms with the Deliverer?

....

CRISIS IN GILEAD

Jephthah's brothers, apparently unable to arouse reliable allies from the other tribes and neighbors, went to the trouble and expense to travel to Tob and locate him. Based upon his reputation as a warrior, if not their own past conflicts with him, they proposed to obtain his services as a leader, and initiate a defensive military response to the imminent Ammonite aggression. Gilead's location on the border of Ammon made them especially vulnerable to attack, and of all the Israelites, most likely to suffer casualties and property losses as soon as Ammonite first strikes would begin.

CRISIS OF FAMILY RESTORATION

Negotiation began on an unfriendly note. Jephthah immediately questioned their motives, reminding them "Did not ye hate me, and expel me out of my father's house? and why are ye come unto me now when ye are in distress?" (Judges 11: 7)

His brothers lost no time making the offer that, if he would come to their aid, they would acknowledge him as "head over all the inhabitants of Gilead." (Judges 11: 8)

JEPHTHAH'S DOUBT

Jephthah was not inclined to get involved. He had no doubt that they needed his help, but questioned whether they were being forthright in offering him a permanent leadership position. The way he worded it is significant: "If you bring me home again to fight against the children of Ammon, and the Lord deliver them before me, shall I be your head?" (11: 9)

THE TURNING POINT

He could have put his own interests first, but his wording reveals his heart of faith. Living in Tob, he had made a name as a freelance marauder, a pal of "vain" fellows. Now, he makes no demand for reinstatement. He repeated their proposition with an amendment, "and the Lord deliver them before me…" (11:9)

This was the turning point in the talks. His brothers followed his lead, appealing to their highest authority, "The Lord be witness between us, if we do not so according to thy words." (Judges 11:10)

Bringing the Lord into the conversation not only acknowledged God's sovereignty, but it affirmed their willingness to submit to the Lord's jurisdiction, by declaring Him a "witness" to their commitment. They could have employed human witnesses to their contract, as was commonly done. For example, human witnesses sealed the contract utilized by Boaz a few years later (Ruth 4: 7-9).

THE LORD IS OUR WITNESS

The Bible's first use of the term "galeed" gives it a specific meaning. It was the term from which the family and regional name "Gilead" came. When Jacob entered his final agreement and cessation of hostilities with Uncle Laban, he erected a pillar and a stack of stones, which Jacob called "Galeed," meaning "heap of witness" (Genesis 31: 45-48).

When Gilead's sons called upon the Lord to be witness to their agreement with Jephthah, they were inviting God's judgment upon them if they did not honor the covenant contract they were making.

HIS EYE IS ON THE SPARROW

Unlike the prodigal's brother in Jesus' parable, Jephthah's brothers wholeheartedly invited their brother to come home, and more than that, to take the place of honor in the family. If he had known the Psalm (which was yet to be written), Jephthah might have sung. "Yea, the sparrow hath found an house, and the swallow a nest for herself, where she may lay her young, even thine altars, O Lord of hosts, my King and my God." (Psalm 84:3)

Indeed, God does take thought for lowly sparrows (Matthew 10:29-31). "The Lord is merciful and gracious… He hath not dealt with us after our sins; nor rewarded us according to our iniquities." (Psalm 103: 8,10) Jephthah, the son of an harlot, rejected by his own family, must have realized that day, if never before, that the Lord God of Israel was actively at work in his life, willing to bless him.

TRUE FAMILY RECONCILIATION

This was more than a reconciliation of convenience for the family. The brothers invoked the Lord as Witness to their promise. Then "the people made him head and captain over them" (Judges 11:11). They all returned to the family estate in

Mizpeh of Gilead and formally inaugurated Jephthah as their captain. And, Jephthah's demeanor at this holy assembly was unlike it would have been during his exile in Tob. He humbly "uttered all his words before the Lord in Mizpeh." (11: 11)

Mizpeh is another name (like galeed) which Jacob gave the place where he erected the pillar and stones of witness when he contracted the mutual promise with Uncle Laban that they would not do each other harm (Genesis 31: 48-52).

Jephthah moved his family back from Tob to the family home at Mizpeh[16] at that time. It is stated shortly afterward that he returned to his home there after his decisive battle with the Ammonites (Judges 11:34).

THE VALUE OF HISTORY

Although about seven centuries had passed since Jacob named Mizpeh, all of this history was well known to Jephthah and to all of Israel. In the next segment of the story (Judges 11:12-28), Jephthah recounted in great detail the events that factored into his contention that the Ammonites had no legal right to possess the land that was being contested. He appealed to a virtual statute of limitations, when he demanded an explanation of why the Ammonites had never forced Israel out of the contested region for a period of 300 years (11:26).[17]

PEACE NEGOTIATIONS

Jephthah sent messengers to appeal to the King of Ammon, asking why he had intruded into Gilead spoiling for a fight. The King claimed that Israel had taken the land from Ammon many years earlier. His response was an ultimatum: he wanted those lands "restored peaceably."

Military couriers went back and forth, presenting Jephthah's diplomatic argument that the land properly belonged to Israel. He asserted that "The Lord God of Israel delivered... and smote... So now the Lord God of Israel hath dispossessed the Amorites... So whomsoever the Lord our God shall drive out from before us, them we will possess." (11:21,23,24)

INVOKING THE LORD

Finally, Jephthah summarized the situation, "I have not sinned against thee, but thou doest me wrong to war against me: the Lord the Judge be judge this day between the children of Israel and the children of Ammon." (Judges 11:27)

Invoking the Lord as Deliverer and Judge is more evidence that Jephthah was no longer operating as he had as a gang leader in Tob. Something had happened in his heart. These are not the arrogant words of a self-absorbed outlaw. These are words of faith!

REJECTION, RESTORATION, RECONCILIATION

Scripture exacts the pivotal point: "Then the Spirit of the Lord came upon Jephthah..." (Judges 11:29) Rejection became restoration when the Holy Spirit approved the family reconciliation. The Holy Spirit "came upon" him with supernatural power to accomplish God's will. This is the kind of power and boldness that sincere faith requisitions.

The rest of verse twenty-nine is a whirlwind of activity, as the once-rejected outcast is transformed into a laser-focused spiritual leader, gathering troops from among the people of Mizpeh in Gilead, and quickly invading Ammonite territory.

The cyclonic energy that emanated from Jephthah in verse twenty-nine demonstrates the amazing speed with which God will remedy our most difficult circumstances when we submit to Him.

EMPOWERMENT IS AVAILABLE

The captain was supercharged with spiritual power when God's people abandoned their petty quarrel.

Everything works when God empowers it. Nothing works as long as we cling to earthly values and fleshly prejudice. Empowerment is readily available to believers, but the firing pin is released by a choice, an act of the will, as we shall see.

....

THE TRANSFORMING CHOICE

The biography of Jephthah (Judges 11: 1-12:7) contains features common to many life stories: foolish parental choices, bullying, sibling rivalry, family conflict, rejection, escape, estrangement, exile, bad friends, and poor reputation. Then comes the crisis that brings factions back together to resist a common enemy. Even the cohesion that developed around the once-rejected hero is not uncommon.

The thing that makes this story unique is the very thing that is often misunderstood and criticized. Jephthah made a choice. The controversial choice that made him a key Bible character is his decision to make a vow. That is the topic that is almost universally avoided:

"And Jephthah vowed a vow unto the Lord, and said, If thou shalt without fail deliver the children of Ammon into mine hands, Then it shall be, that whatsoever cometh forth of the doors of my house to meet me, when I return in peace from the children of Ammon, shall surely be the Lord's, and I will offer it up for a burnt offering." (Judges 11: 30-31)

Those who are critical must admit that this so-called "foolish vow" was linked to the Spirit coming upon him, as shown by the sequence of the context (Judges 11: 29-30).

THE LORD'S RESPONSE

When God's servants make stringent, honest vows to Him, the Lord responds. But, it is doubtful that any heartfelt vow is ever made without the one making the vow realizing his indebtedness to the Lord for His abundant blessings.

Some have described Jacob's vow at Bethel (the first time the term vow is used in Scripture) as a conditional vow: "If God will be with me, and will keep me in this way that I go… So that I come again to my father's house in peace, then shall the Lord be my God" (Genesis 28: 20-21).

The idea that Jacob's vow is conditional hinges on his use of "if." But, the "if" in Jacob's vow, like many other "ifs" in the Bible, may be understood to be "since."[18] Jacob was not bargaining with God, but rather, acknowledging His boundless provision and presence. He was saying, "If, and it is true, God will be with me…"

BOLD CONFIDENCE

When Jephthah vowed to sacrifice "whatsoever cometh forth of the doors of my house to meet me," (11: 31) he was sure that God's blessing was upon his plan. He was willing to make a sacrifice equal to the Lord's expected empowerment. He fully anticipated a victorious return. The Spirit infused him with confidence, a presentiment of the Apostles' dauntlessness: "when they saw the boldness of Peter and John…they marveled…" (Acts 4: 13)

And, the Lord responded to faith in his heart! "So Jephthah passed over to the children of Ammon to fight against them; and the Lord delivered them into his hands. And he smote them from Aroer, even till thou come to Minnith, even twenty cities, and unto the plain of the vineyards, with a very great slaughter. Thus the children of Ammon were subdued before the children of Israel." (Judges 11: 32-33) The victory was phenomenal! They cut a wide circular swath conquering twenty cities.

Be sure, the Lord will respond to you, when you take seriously His will and His willingness to bless you.

·····································

THE LORD'S REQUIREMENT

The Lord wants to empower us to keep our vows, but He is very specific that vows are serious. Jephthah knew the Lord's viewpoint on voluntary vows.

During Jephthah's lifetime, Job and the Pentateuch, the first five books of our Bible, known as the books of Moses, was available. Joshua's history detailing conquest of the land had also been written. Jephthah's knowledge of Israel's history, used in negotiations with Ammon's king, show that he was very competent in this knowledge.

THE BOOKS OF MOSES

If he was only familiar with the books of Moses, he knew the guidelines for vows in Numbers 30. Women, as well as men, were permitted to make vows to the Lord. Women could vow if they wished, but fathers of single women and husbands of married women had the right—indeed, the obligation—to veto a vow. However, if a father or husband did not veto the vow of a woman, she was as obliged to fulfill the vow as a man, in which case the duty fell upon the father or husband to enable her to keep the vow as if he had made the vow himself.

HANNAH'S VOW

Some years after Jephthah's lifetime, but still within the period of the Judges, Samuel's mother, Hannah, made a vow to God. She was barren and childless, but she promised that if the Lord gave her a son, she would dedicate him to the Lord's service from the time he was weaned. Her husband did not disallow the vow, so it stood. God granted her request, and she kept her vow. This was a heart- rending obligation to keep, giving up her toddler to grow up at the tabernacle with Eli's family.

Samuel became the most effective of all the Judges of Israel, preaching revivals, writing four books of the Bible, and anointing two kings of Israel. And, God blessed Hannah, too. Her prayer of thanksgiving was preserved for all time, and she bore five more children.

LEVITICUS AND DEUTERONOMY

Leviticus detailed how sacrifices were to be offered in the fulfilling of vows. Deuteronomy was also very direct: "When thou shalt vow a vow unto the Lord thy God, thou shalt not slack to pay it: for the Lord thy God will surely require it of thee; and it would be sin in thee. But if thou shalt forbear to vow, it shall be no sin in thee. That which is gone out of thy lips thou shalt keep and perform; even a freewill offering, according as thou hast vowed unto the Lord thy God, which thou hast promised with thy mouth." (Deuteronomy 23: 21-23)

Although Jephthah died before the time of David, the writings of David and Solomon demonstrate that the principles governing vows remained the same during their kingdom years as it had been since the time of Moses. In fact, those guidelines seem to have already been understood before the time of Moses, practiced by Abraham and Jacob more than four centuries before

Moses lived. There may be reason to believe that many of the basic principles were understood and practiced by Adam and taught to his descendants, through men like Enoch and Noah, who lived not long before Abraham and Job.

DAVID, ASAPH, HEZEKIAH & SOLOMON

The psalms are songs used for centuries at the tabernacle and in the temple. Many of them speak of vows, showing that Israel was constantly reminded of the blessing and privilege of making vows to the Lord. David mentions them in Psalm 22: 25, 56: 12, 61: 5,8, 65: 1, and 132: 2. Asaph, Hezekiah and others included the topic in Psalm 50: 14, 66: 13, 76: 11, and 116: 14. A study of these psalms yields invaluable teaching about vowing vows.

Solomon, the wisest man, expanded the Kingdom to its greatest reach, and taught about vows too. Many still memorize Solomon's version of Moses' admonition in Deuteronomy 23: "When thou vowest a vow unto God, defer not to pay it; for he hath no pleasure in fools: pay that which thou hast vowed. Better is it that thou shouldest not vow, than that thou shouldest vow and not pay. Suffer not thy mouth to cause thy flesh to sin; neither say thou before the angel, that it was an error: wherefore should God be angry at thy voice, and destroy the work of thine hands?" (Ecclesiastes 5: 4-6)

It is true that a vow is no trifling matter. But, vows made in faith invite God's blessing in abundance, as our next chapter explains.

"For thou, O God, hast heard my vows: thou hast given me the heritage of those that fear thy name."

—David (Psalm 61: 5)

....

VOLUNTARY HOLY VOWS

When God's servants make willing vows with holy motives, the Lord is pleased because such vows are made in faith. For "whatsoever is not of faith is sin" (Romans 14: 23) and "without faith it is impossible to please him" (Hebrews 11: 6).

Nobody is able to fulfill vows, even if they are made in faith, without God's continuing provision of health, strength, financial resources, and other considerations.

RELIGION & VOWS

One would think that religion would champion a fellow who made a vow to God. After all, religious orders are known for taking vows. Other than a funeral, the most common religious ceremony known to man—the wedding—is centered upon the taking of vows.

But, cheerleaders on Jephthah's team are few. Some think Jephthah was foolish to make this vow. Many think that his was the kind of vow that Solomon warned against: "Better is it that thou shouldest not vow, than that thou shouldest vow and not pay. Suffer not thy mouth to cause thy flesh to sin; neither say thou before the angel, that it was an error: wherefore should God be angry at thy voice, and destroy the work of thine hands."

(Ecclesiastes 5: 5-6) Many Bible teachers avoid Jephthah's story, and many who comment on it seem to miss the point.

Notice that Solomon is not warning against the making of vows, but only of failing to pay what is vowed. Jephthah seems to have correctly understood that once a vow is made to God, there is no turning back. It is absolutely required.

Jephthah's faith was honored. God reimbursed him by giving him a resounding victory over the Ammonites. The Bible gives many parallel examples: Daniel believed God and kept praying in defiance of the King's edict. He was delivered from the lion's den and the King acknowledged God's sovereignty. By faith, Philip left the revival at Samaria, obeying the Lord's leading to a lonely stretch of the Gaza road, where God led him to speak to one man who turned out to be the Treasurer of Ethiopia. What a reimbursement for his faith!

DO BIBLE SCHOLARS MISS THE POINT?

The New Bible Commentary says, "This… statement that he did with her according to his vow is best taken as implying her actual sacrifice. Although human sacrifice was strictly forbidden to Israelites, we need not be surprised at a man of Jephthah's half-Canaanite antecedents following Canaanite usage in this matter."[19]

How does this claim that Jephthah's antecedents were "half-Canaanite" go unchallenged? Nothing in the text verifies that his harlot mother was of Canaanite ancestry, although she might have been. Beside that, there is no statement that she had any influence upon him, although it could be so. The comment seems dismissive.

A Cambridge scholar blames Jephthah's supposed human sacrifice on a lack of vitality in faithful practice of the Levitical priesthood: "The religious system of Israel had fallen into suspension. From the days of Phinehas… to the time of Samuel, we hear nothing of the high priest, the ark or the tabernacle."[20]

Since the period of Judges stretched over 400 years, it is difficult to imagine how the Levitical system could have survived and recovered the strength it had during the time of Samuel and David, after such a long hiatus as the Cambridge scholar implies. Hannah and her family seem to have been faithful attendants at Tabernacle events, and Eli's sons lived "high on the hog" from the bountiful sacrifices of the Israelites. That would hardly argue for a system that had "fallen into suspension."

MORE AMBIGUITY

The Amplified Bible, relegates Jephthah's vow to greater ambiguity by providing footnotes from several commentaries, noting that "Scholars fail to agree as to what Jephthah really did… the fact that the maidens mourned her virginity and not her death seems to prove that she did not die."[21]

As a young pastor forty years ago, the author gave a series of Sunday night messages from the book of Judges. In ignorance I preached that Jephthah offered his daughter in human sacrifice. Although fascinated with the story, I was uncomfortable about the implications. But, my best resources seemed to say that Jephthah had likely offered his daughter as a burnt sacrifice in order to keep his vow to God. Some commentaries saw it as a tragic example of the ignorance and barbarity of the times of the Judges.

RATIONALIZING ABOUT VOWS

A lesser man than Jephthah might have equivocated on the terms of his vow. Who has not pondered the option of "borrowing" the tithe or missions commitment money for a week or two? "God understands," we rationalize. "Money is tight right now." Had Jephthah been of lesser character, the legendary story of his vow, his once-in-a-lifetime opportunity, and his eternal reward might have been jettisoned in the confusion of intellectual deliberation.

Let us consider that it is vitally important that scripture makes it plain that Jephthah did indeed honor his vow, despite the consequences.

····································

BROKEN VOWS

While Jephthah's life challenges us to make holy vows, since faith pleases God (Hebrews 11: 6), a conversation about the Biblical view of vows leads us to admit that we live in a fallen, sinful world, where vows of all kinds are almost universally broken.

BROKEN MARITAL VOWS

The Lord Jesus made the point concerning marital vows, in His Sermon on the Mount (Matthew 5: 27-32). Adultery, after all, is one of the primary ways in which people break the Ten Commandments.[22]

Jesus connected the dots for us, explaining that hatred is paramount to murder, and the lustful look is tantamount to adultery (Matthew 5: 21-22,27-32). Murder and adultery are two common tests people fall back on, attempting to prove they are righteous. Often the protest is voiced, "but, I've never murdered anybody!"

But, Jesus said, "except your righteousness shall exceed the righteousness of the scribes and Pharisees, ye shall in no case enter into the kingdom of heaven." (Matthew 5: 20)

HATRED EQUALS MURDER

Explaining the interconnection of anger, hatred and murder, Jesus said that calling one's brother, "Thou fool,"—an offense that to us would seem less serious than hatred—would put us "in danger of hell fire." (5: 22)

In other words, Jesus raised the bar, making lust, anger, and hatred offenses that disqualify us for Heaven, and qualify us for Hell!

The point is, no human being can keep the law (the ten commandments). James says, "whosoever shall keep the whole law, and yet offend in one point, he is guilty of all." (James 2: 10) Paul explains, "the law was our schoolmaster to bring us to Christ, that we might be justified by faith." (Galatians 3: 24) The Commandments set the bar so high that no human, except Christ Himself (Matthew 5: 17) can pass the test. Our only hope is to trust Christ, our Substitute and Redeemer.

KEEPING THE COMMANDMENTS

The Rich Young Ruler, like many religious people today, bragged that he had kept all the commandments since childhood (Matthew 19: 16-22). Jesus listed six of the ten, including adultery as second in his list. When the young man claimed innocence, Jesus turned the spotlight on his failure to live without covetousness, by challenging him to "sell that thou hast, and give to the poor… " This demonstrated his reluctance to part with his possessions, which was equivalent to coveting, breaking the tenth and the second commandments. After all, the possessions we have are not ours. They belong to God. We are only managers.

APPLICATION TO JEPHTHAH

Application of this truth must include the matter of vows. Indeed, man's propensity to break his commitments is what makes Jephthah's story so compelling! Someone who actually does keep a vow demonstrates integrity that is beyond the ordinary in human experience. All the quibbling about how Jephthah kept his vow distracts from the fact that he really did keep his vow!

PHARISEES WALK AWAY

Pharisees are satisfied to celebrate the 50th wedding anniversary, as if achievement of this milestone verifies that the couple never broke their wedding vows. Jesus' standard would inquire into the heart of the matter: were either of the couple guilty of looking with lust? This is why the scribes and Pharisees all walked away rather than execute the woman caught in adultery (John 8: 9). Jesus specified that only someone "without sin." is qualified to cast the first stone (v.7).

Truth demands execution for those who hate or lust, not just for murderers and adulterers (Ezekiel 18: 20). But, thank God, grace forgives the repentant offender, based upon the blood sacrifice of a sinless lamb (John 1: 29).

NO LICENSE TO SIN

This is not to advocate the breaking of vows, or to provide license to sin, but to acknowledge that the best human vow-keeping falls short of the glory of God (Romans 3: 23). Our best righteousness is as filthy rags in God's economy (Isaiah 64: 6).

We live in a real world that is decimated by broken vows. Jephthah's father is not the only man who ever visited a harlot. Jephthah is not the only son who found the pressures of family relationships too unforgiving. Certainly, he is not the only one who found an excuse to become a prodigal in the far country.

PRETENDING OR ADMITTING

We can maintain our superiority, like scribes and Pharisees, pretending that our standards are just as high as God's. We can murmur about parties for prodigals, and pride ourselves in our perfect record of attendance, external compliance, and dead works (Luke 15: 25-29, Hebrews 6: 1, 9: 14). Or, we can join broken-hearted prodigals and publicans who admit their sinfulness and plead for mercy and grace from a compassionate Father. (Luke 15: 18- 21, 18: 13, Psalm 103: 8-14, Isaiah 61: 1, Luke 4: 18)

THE TWENTY-YEAR VOW

It would be disingenuous for me to speak of broken vows as if I have no personal experience. Many years ago, I was invited to candidate for the pastorate of a church that had survived some serious problems. During the process, I was very forthright about my preferences, convictions, and intentions about the ministry, if I were to come. Despite the fact that I set up some major hurdles, the church called us, and we went.

I had heard that Dr. Ed Nelson had told South Sheridan Baptist Church in Denver that if they called him, he would plan to stay twenty years. This vow he kept, finally resigning on his thirtieth anniversary, after three amazing decades. Dr. Nelson had been my pastor, and I admired the integrity that caused him to keep the promise. In the heat of the moment, I made the same commitment of twenty years in a rather off-handed way to the church in Casper. There was no contract as such, and nobody there reminded me of it. But, I could not forget.

ONLY FIVE YEARS

The economics and circumstances that led to my resignation after only five and one-half years could be replayed for those who might listen. But, the point is that my departure did not turn out well for the church, for my family, nor for the church to which I moved. Lost momentum was never regained.

Since then, I often pondered the words and context of Ecclesiastes 5: 5-6 "Better is it that thou shouldest not vow, than that thou shouldest vow and not pay. Suffer not thy mouth to cause thy flesh to sin; neither say thou before the angel, that it was an error: wherefore should God be angry at thy voice, and destroy the work of thine hands?"

OUR WORK DESTROYED

God holds us accountable for vows spoken. The angel mentioned seems to be a reference to a guardian angel (Matthew 18: 10) who will bear testimony as an eyewitness in God's Court to the very words we have spoken. Our Lord Jesus predicted that we will give account of "every idle word." (Matthew 12: 36) If our idle words are under scrutiny, certainly the promises we make are a matter of record, indicating our accountability for failure to keep our vows, but also in view of reward for our successes in retaining the integrity to fulfill them (Matthew 10: 41-42).

At the Bema Seat Judgment (II Corinthians 5: 10-11), believers will be held to account. It will not do to plead, "It was an error." God will be angry with those who attempt such a defense, and will "destroy the work of [our] hands." This judgment scenario is further described by Paul, "Every man's work shall be made manifest: for the day shall declare it, because it shall be revealed by fire; and the fire shall try every man's work of what sort it is. If any man's work abide which he hath built thereupon, he shall receive a reward. If any man's work shall be burned, he shall suffer loss: but he himself shall be saved; yet so as by fire." (I Corinthians 3: 13-15)

NO EXCUSES

Believers must take care to confess failed vows. They must not be whitewashed as mere sins of error. They must be acknowledged as the secret faults, presumptuous sins, or addictions (dominion) that they are (Psalm 19: 12-13). Blaming, making excuses and minimizing will be unacceptable in God's courtroom. The consuming fire of our Lord's gaze will destroy our works (Hebrews 10: 26, 12:28-29, Revelation 1:14), which otherwise might have been rewarded.

GRACIOUS DESTRUCTION

The Lord is gracious to permit our works to be destroyed during our lifetime so we will realize our need to seek true repentance, which only He can grant (Acts 11: 18, II Corinthians 7: 9-10).

Many families and individuals were damaged and still suffer because of the decision I made to break my vow to God and the church at Casper. Let me acknowledge how my choice affected one family.

MICHAEL AND PAM DOYLE

One of the most loyal men of integrity that I have ever worked with was Michael Doyle. He was principal of our Christian school in Casper, a teacher applauded universally by his students for the past thirty years, an underpaid staff member, soul-winner, and unparalleled captain of a Sunday school bus route. He held a bachelor's degree from the University of Wyoming, and a master's from Perdue. Much of our success in youth work in Casper will accrue to his eternal reward. His wife quietly worked a menial job, endured substandard housing, made the best of an inadequate income, and served in church ministries too.

Because of my broken vow, the church went several months without a pastor. Transitions were difficult, coming at a time when families were moving away because of job losses in the oil field. Before long, the school closed. The Doyle family eventually relocated to Virginia, where Mike became a faculty member of two different colleges. But the Christian school movement, and many families in Wyoming were irreversibly affected because the pastor made an impetuous decision to violate a vow concerning God's work. I pray that God in mercy will visit those families.

But, moving on, let us consider what exactly, did Jephthah vow to do?

HUMAN SACRIFICE?

Well informed of Israel's specific history, Jephthah offered convincing legal arguments in the border dispute with the King of Ammon. His thorough knowledge of the details of Israel's history had to have been drawn from the books of Moses and Joshua. Is it even possible that Jephthah could have failed to realize that human sacrifice was forbidden by the Law of Moses? What are the chances that his contemporaries would have failed to point out such an error? Not a chance! Human sacrifice was a Capital crime.

THE IDOL-GOD MOLECH

In Leviticus, the laws of various offerings, essential to the proper worship of Jehovah, were explained:

"And thou shalt not let any of thy seed pass through the fire to Molech..." (Leviticus 18: 21)

"Whosoever he be of the children of Israel, or of the strangers that sojourn in Israel, that giveth any of his seed unto Molech; he shall surely be put to death: the people of the land shall stone him with stones. And I will set my face against that man, and will cut him off from among his people; because he hath given his seed unto Molech, to defile my sanctuary, and to profane my holy name. And if the people of the land do any ways hide their eyes from the man, when he giveth his seed unto Molech, and kill him not: Then I will set my face against that man, and against his family, and will cut him off, and all that go a whoring after him, to commit whoredom with Molech, from among their people." (Leviticus 20: 2-5)

"Take heed to thyself that thou be not snared by following them, after that they be destroyed from before thee; and that thou inquire not after their gods, saying, How did these nations serve their gods?... Thou shalt not do so unto the Lord thy God: for every abomination to the Lord, which he hateth, have they done unto their gods; for even their sons and their daughters they have burnt in the fire to their gods." (Deuteronomy 12:30-31)

CHILD SACRIFICE IS DEMONIC

The practice of child sacrifice was linked to other demonic practices such as divination, enchantment, witchcraft, and communicating with the dead.

"There shall not be found among you any one that maketh his son or his daughter to pass through the fire, or that useth divination, or an observer of times, or an enchanter, or a witch, Or a charmer, or a consulter with familiar spirits or a wizard, or a necromancer. For all that do these things are an abomination unto the Lord:" (Deuteronomy 18: 10-12)

The worship of the Ammonite god, Molech (also called Moloch, Milcom, Malcham), featured "gruesome orgies in which little ones were sacrificed."[23] Moses warned against this religion before Israel entered the promise land. The "image of the god was heated and the bodies of children... were placed in its arms."[24] Later, Solomon allowed his heathen wives to bring with them idol worship of Molech and Chemosh, and to set up "high places" for their worship on Mount Olivet, just outside Jerusalem (I Kings 11: 7,33).

These religions were in operation during Jephthah's time. He challenged the Ammonite King to look to the idol- god Chemosh, a god of Moab[25] to provide blessings to Ammon, rather than taking land provided to Israel by Jehovah (Judges 11:24). Moab and Ammon descended from Lot's daughters, who were irreparably influenced by the evil practices of Sodom. (Genesis19) It is no surprise that the nations that descended from them adopted abominable practices, including child sacrifice.

KING MESHA'S CHILD SACRIFICE

The Moabite King Mesha offered his eldest son, who was the heir to his throne, in a burnt sacrifice to Chemosh because his army lost a war against Ahab's son, Jehoram. (II Kings 3: 4-27) Mesha's version of the sacrifice, without acknowledging his defeat, was inscribed on the Moabite stone, discovered by a missionary in 1868, and eventually housed in the Louvre in Paris.[26]

The main worship center for Molech and Chemosh, during Israel's later history under King Manasseh (long after Solomon and Ahab) was the valley of the son of Hinnom (II Chronicles 33: 6), which became known as Gehenna. Jesus used this place as a type of Hell (Matthew 5: 29-30).[27] Jeremiah said they had "filled this place with the blood of innocents…" (Jeremiah 7: 9-11, 19:2-13)

As wicked as the Israelites were during the times of the Judges, their compromise with these evil practices became more prevalent during the final years before they went into captivity. Ezekiel (23: 37-39) spoke out, indicting the Jews for attending child sacrifice and coming to the temple on the same day.

The writer of Psalm 106, reviewing how God's people forgot the Lord's blessing, noted, "They… mingled among the heathen, and learned their works. And they served their idols: which were a snare unto them. Yea, they sacrificed their sons and their daughters unto devils, and shed innocent blood, even the blood of their sons and of their daughters, whom they sacrificed unto the idols of Canaan: and the land was polluted with blood. Thus were they defiled with their own works, and went a whoring with their own inventions. Therefore was the wrath of the Lord kindled against his people, insomuch that he abhorred his own inheritance." (Psalm 106: 34-40)

PIOUS, BUT UNENLIGHTENED?

One commentary, ignoring Jephthah's thorough knowledge of Israel's history, admits he was pious but unenlightened: "there is but too much reason to conclude that he was impelled to the fulfillment [of his vow] by the dictates of a pious but unenlightened conscience." [28]

Dr. John MacArthur concurs, commenting on "the pain felt by her father in having to take the life of his only daughter to satisfy his pious, but unwise pledge." [29]

It seems strange that he was pious enough to have instant recall of scriptural history and loyal enough to feel compelled to fulfill his vow, but without conscience to the extent of practicing a human sacrifice of his only child.

Why would Samuel the human author, not to mention the Holy Spirit, neglect to comment on such overt ignorance or disobedience to the dictates of the Law of Moses?

Even during one of the darkest of times in Israel's history, disclosed in Judges 19-20, when a Levite's concubine "played the whore," (19: 2), was grossly abused, and murdered by some

Benjamites, "the congregation was gathered together as one man, from Dan even to Beersheba, with the land of Gilead, unto the Lord in Mizpeh. And the chief of all the people, even of all the tribes of Israel, presented themselves in the assembly of the people of God, four hundred thousand footmen that drew sword." (Judges 20: 1-3)

ONE OF ISRAEL'S DARKEST HOURS

This assembly of 400,000 met to inquire, "Tell us, how was this wickedness?" (Judges 20: 3) Two chapters account for the awful wickedness into which Israel descended during the period of Judges. It bears witness to the fact that, even at its worst, all the tribes of Israel, including those east of Jordan (like Jephthah's people) still remained loyal to called tabernacle gatherings, and had a united conscience about practices to be viewed as absolutely reprehensible.

Martin Luther, who translated Scripture into German from the Hebrew, observes, "it does not 'stand there in the text,' that she was offered in sacrifice."[30]

Was Jephthah pious but unenlightened? To say so begs disregard to a detailed familiarity with the text.

CHILD SACRIFICE TODAY?

Abortion is, for most who practice it, the sacrifice of one's child in order to enjoy sexual and financial freedom from responsibility. Thus, abortion is today's version of sacrifice of innocent lives to the gods of money and sensuality.

But, what did Jephthah actually do?

"It would have been next to impossible for Jephthah to have found a priest who would perform such a sacrifice." [31]

—Warren Baker

....

SO WHAT HAPPENED TO THE GIRL?

Did Jephthah offer his daughter as a burnt sacrifice to Jehovah God? The question must be faced if we are to understand the intent, the interpretation, and the proper application of the scriptural passage.

If he did, why does the Bible seem to lift him to the status of hero? He is even mentioned in the roster of "The Hall of Faith." (Hebrews 11: 32) And, there is no other Jephthah or Jephthae in all of scripture, who might have been the one referenced here.

THE GREATEST SACRIFICE

No doubt, he dedicated her to remain a virgin, never bearing children. In so doing, he sacrificed something that no Middle-eastern man, then or now, would have wanted. Perhaps a man's greatest fear in that culture is to have no son to carry on his name.

ABRAM, SARAI, & HAGAR

Abram and Sarai were past the age of child-bearing. Growing weary of waiting for God to fulfill His promise of a son, she devised a plan to "help God." Sarai would give her Egyptian handmaiden, Hagar, to Abram. When she gave birth, the child would be legally considered to be Sarai's child as well as Abram's. Hagar would continue to serve in her current role as a servant. After all, as a slave, she lived only to fulfill the wishes of her master and mistress.

The Bible says that Abram "hearkened to the voice of Sarai" (Genesis 16: 2), which is more than a little reminiscent of Adam falling for Eve's idea of eating the forbidden fruit.

Sarai's plan did not work out so well. Hagar gave birth to the child, Ishmael. Life in the family returned to normal, except that now Hagar seemed to feel she was worthy of higher status. Not that she ever said so; it was just a feeling Sarai had. Sarai began to complain to Abram about the servant girl's insolent attitude, "when she saw that she had conceived, I was despised in her eyes…" (Genesis16: 5)

THE BARREN WIFE

The problem of the barren wife surfaces often in scripture: Rachel was the favored wife, unable to conceive, but Leah, the unchosen wife, who was forced upon Jacob by his father-in-law, bore children prolifically.

Elkanah loved Hannah, but she was barren. His other wife, Peninah had no problem conceiving, and no problem reminding Hannah of her inability to get pregnant. "And her adversary also provoked her sore, for to make her fret, because the Lord had shut up her womb." (I Samuel 1: 6)

NO SON TO PRESERVE HIS NAME

Jephthah is the most famous man of his generation. He had pals in the land of Tob, but we don't know any of their names.

His brothers, the other sons of Gilead, remain unnamed in the historical record. Even the King of Ammon, Jephthah's enemy, is only referred to by his title. We don't know his name. During their pre-battle negotiations, Jephthah mentions names of earlier kings in the region, including Sihon, Balak, and Zippor. No other name of Jephthah's contemporary generation is preserved. Even his daughter's name is not given, although other writers, in dramatizing the story, have named her.

THE NAME OF HIS DAUGHTER

Jephthah's daughter was given the name Seila in the writings of Pseudo Philo, and the Masonic Lodge-related Order of the Eastern Star refers to her as Adah. George Buchanan, the Scottish scholar and dramatist (1506-1582) "called her Iphis, obviously alluding to Iphigenia" (from Greek Mythology's Agamemnon, to whom she is often compared). George Frederick Handel used the same name (Iphis) in his 1751 oratorio Jephtha, which was based on Buchanan's play.[32] These treatments, like Josephus, assume that she was offered in human sacrifice.[33]

JEPHTHAH'S TRIUMPHANT RETURN

When Jephthah had won the war against Ammon, he returned from battle. The Bible says, "And Jephthah came to Mizpeh unto his house, and, behold, his daughter came out to meet him with timbrels and with dances: and she was his only child; beside her he had neither son nor daughter. And it came to pass, when he saw her, that he rent his clothes, and said, Alas, my daughter! thou hast brought me very low, and thou art one of them that trouble me: for I have opened my mouth unto the Lord, and I cannot go back." (Judges 11: 34-35)

Away with this crowd of Bible scholars who say that Jephthah was a crude, barbaric product of his times, a virtual caveman who had so little understanding of the Mosaic Law that he would perform a human sacrifice, thinking that in so doing he would please Jehovah!

The passionate words of this man who had a deep- seated spiritual conviction about a vow he made to the Lord are these: "I have opened my mouth unto the Lord, and I cannot go back." (Judges 11: 35)

THE HOLY SPIRIT'S WORDING

Even the Holy Spirit's choice of wording, as He used Samuel the Prophet to write this story instructs us, using the surprise word "behold," so frequently employed in Scripture at crucial times. The writer might have yelled, "Pay attention! This is important!"

Zodiates observes, "if he had intended a human sacrifice, why would he have been so surprised and distraught when his daughter became the object of the vow (v.35)?" and, "he knew that sacrifices to Jehovah were to be exclusively of the male gender (v.34)" and, "it would have been next to impossible for Jephthah to have found a priest who would perform such a sacrifice."[34]

THE OVERLOOKED CLUE

The end of the sentence provides the clue that so many have ignored: "and she was his only child; beside her he had neither son nor daughter." (Judges 11: 34)

Jephthah had made a holy vow to God. He had been a prodigal, but had made the decision to come home, to be reunited with his brothers. When he agreed to risk life and limb in defense of the family estate and the heritage of the Lord given to Israel and the tribe of Manasseh, he had "uttered all his words before the Lord in Mizpeh." (Judges 11: 11)

He knew what God's Word said about the making of a vow, and that it forbad human sacrifice. He knew that he had made a commitment that had ensnared him by the words of his mouth. It was a matter of honor. It was a matter of holiness.

WHAT DID HE EXPECT?

The Bible doesn't tell us what Jephthah expected when he got home. His vow was to sacrifice, "whatsoever cometh forth of the doors of my house to meet me" (Judges 11: 31). The Hebrew word deleth (doors) signifies "something swinging… (two leaved), gate, leaf, lid…" which can be understood as a reference to the entrance gate to his home. The same word appears in Psalm 141: 3 "Set a watch, O Lord, before my mouth; keep the door of my lips."[35]

This broadens the possibilities of what the warrior might have reasonably anticipated.

It may be that, like the man in the Prophet Nathan's story, Jephthah's family had a pet lamb, as many certainly did. A "little ewe lamb, which he had bought and nourished up: and it grew up together with him and with his children: it did eat of his own meat, and drank of his own cup, and lay in his bosom, and was unto him as a daughter." (II Samuel 12: 3)

When Nathan told his parable to David, it aroused feelings that took the old King back to his childhood—back to the quiet days of shepherding, which he had enjoyed so much as a lad. Maybe the Prophet knew that David had once had just such a little pet lamb. He used the emotion and pathos of the story to press upon the King the guilt of his sins (II Samuel 12: 1-5).

Surely Jephthah never imagined that his own daughter—his only child—would be the first one to come out to meet him upon his return from battle.

THE VOW IN MIZPEH

In Mizpeh, in the heat of the moment, he pondered his earnest desire to do the will of God. He was impassioned to offer to God a vow worthy of the magnanimous favor he was seeking in prayer—the Divine favor upon his battle strategy and the almost unimaginable hope that he might be empowered to win a decisive victory for his family, for his tribe, for Israel and most of all, for the God of Israel.

He was aware of Joshua's prayers before the people marched around Jericho. He could recite the exploits of the left-handed Ehud, of Shamgar and his ox goad, and of Gideon. Was there ever a greater transformation than that which Jehovah had done, bringing the bashful, inferior Gideon to win the most famous battles of his era?

WHAT SHALL I GIVE THEE, MASTER?

In Mizpeh, in the presence of his brothers and men of Manasseh, he had searched his mind, during the emotion-packed prayer meeting. No doubt, the men called upon Jehovah to intervene and give them victory against the encroaching Ammonite hordes.

For days, well-armed messengers made their way back and forth to the Ammonite king's castle. Back in Mizpeh, Jephthah waited pensively, reviewed strategy, heard reports from advance scouts, and consulted with advisors. At stolen intervals, his mind returned to the inner conviction that he ought to make a vow, but what would be an appropriate promise? What should his vow entail?

DIPLOMACY ENDED

Negotiations fell apart. Jephthah's appeal to history fell on deaf ears. Arrogantly, the king of Ammon sent the ambassadors from Manasseh away without a peace plan.

It was time to move!

Jephthah's guerrilla unit, hastily trained, received the secret signal mobilizing early deployment. "We'll mount up and invade Ammon long before daylight."

THE ATTACK

They rendezvoused before dawn outside the village of Aroer. Within minutes they would be in the heat of battle. Who knows? He might be killed in battle. This might be his one opportunity to prove his repentance to everyone…

And then, it came to him. The lamb!

On a recent trip to the tabernacle, he had decided to redeem the lamb. It was a spotless, unblemished specimen.

In his lifetime, he thought he had never seen a finer lamb. Having the lamb appraised, a very high price was declared by the priest who assessed animals to be ransomed. He had gladly added the 20 % to redeem his daughter's pet which was the family's favorite. (Lev. 27: 13,31)

We all make statements and do not realize that circumstances may turn in such a way that we may end up regretting our words. But, believers must consider that God knows the end from the beginning! Nothing is unexpected to Him. When anyone makes a vow, there are unforeseen events that may have a major impact on outcomes before the last chapter is complete.

To vow or not to vow—that is the question that defines the difference between a name remembered, or a name forgotten.

JEPHTHAH'S POSTERITY

There must be more to the story of Jephthah's childhood. Maybe there was a godly daddy or mama who poured oil of gladness and sweetness of contentment into the young boy Jephthah, in spite of the inherent conflicts brought on by his daddy's foolish venture into harlotry. Somebody must have decided to live a life of devotion that made a difference. That difference was transferred to the next generation.

We have no information in the Bible about Jephthah's wife. We can only assume that she was a Jewish girl he knew in his youth and married, supposing he would always remain on the family homestead, raising lambs and lentils. The behavior and attitude seen in the daughter seems to suggest a godly home, the mirror image of her dad's fierce loyalty to principle.

JEPHTHAH'S FATHER DIED

But, Gilead, Jephthah's father, had died. The brothers, who had been whispering behind his back, suddenly rose up and thrust him out of the inheritance: "Thou shalt not inherit in our father's house: for thou art the son of a strange woman." (11: 2)

In confusion, Jephthah's little family fled to Tob. The bitterness of rejection took its toll, and Jephthah pursued a rebel's lifestyle, or at least a life of pleasure. [36] But, while Jephthah ran with a bad crowd, perhaps somebody prayed and wept, begging Jehovah God to bring the offended Jephthah back to the Lord and back to the people of God.

Could it have been his god-fearing wife or his praying stepmother?

Who can absolutely reject the possibility that Jephthah's wife was grieved by the tragic situation—the rejection of her husband by his brothers, and her little family's exile to a gentile town where, like Naomi in the story of Ruth, she had to try to make a new life among heathen, and cope with an angry husband, hurt and disoriented by his undeserved and prejudicial dismissal from the tribe and family.

An only daughter was growing up. Mother told her the stories of Adam and Eve, Noah, Abraham and Sarah, Isaac and Rebekah, Jacob, Rachel, Leah, Joseph, Dinah, and Moses.

Together, mother and daughter memorized and recited Joshua's declaration, "And if it seem evil unto you to serve the Lord, choose you this day whom ye will serve; whether the gods which your fathers served that were on the other side of the flood, or the gods of the Amorites, in whose land ye dwell: but as for me and my house, we will serve the Lord." (Joshua 24: 15)

THE BROTHERS ARRIVED

The sons of Gilead, Jephthah's brothers, rode into Tob. Asking directions, they arrived at Jephthah's home. Nervously, they approached their estranged brother, not knowing that God had prepared his heart. Prayers that they had not uttered had reached the God who had met Jacob at Mizpeh. Jephthah accepted their words of contrition, although he seemed dubious. To their surprise, with little resistance, he agreed to come home.

That night, as Jephthah lay in bed, he admitted it: the real reason he had agreed to return was not his brothers' retractions and apologies. It was the little girl in the next room. He couldn't let her grow up with a daddy who was running from God. He couldn't let her reach adulthood with an outlaw dad whose companions were "vain men."

AMMON LOST THE WAR

And now, it was all history. Ammon was defeated. Jephthah's brothers, true to their word, had proclaimed him head of the clan. Word was spreading fast that Jephthah should be made Judge of all Israel.

Now his sweet daughter faced a dilemma, which had crashed upon them all. This nightmare was upon them because of a vow that nobody had forced upon him.

LIKE ABRAHAM ON MORIAH

Still, Jephthah knew from scripture that the will of Jehovah was better than a thousand descendants. He understood now what Abraham felt as he trudged up Mount Moriah, prepared to sacrifice Isaac, the son of God's Promise.

His mind replayed the cinema of events: "And Jephthah came to Mizpeh unto his house, and behold, his daughter came out to meet him with timbrels and with dances: and she was his only child; beside her he had neither son nor daughter.

"And it came to pass, when he saw her, that he rent his clothes, and said, Alas, my daughter! thou hast brought me very low, and thou art one of them that trouble me: for I have opened my mouth unto the Lord, and I cannot go back.

"And she said unto him, My father, if thou hast opened thy mouth unto the Lord, do to me according to that which hath proceeded out of thy mouth; forasmuch as the Lord hath taken vengeance for thee of thine enemies, even of the children of Ammon." (Judges 11: 34-36)

A SPOILED CHILD?

Does the daughter's response sound like that of a spoiled only-child of a rebellious prodigal, a reject full of bitter resentments, and with no redeeming grace bestowed by the God of all grace?

In the courtyard in front of the cottage in Mizpeh, chickens were clucking. The pet lamb nuzzled his leg. He looked through tearful eyes at the teenage girl.

YOU'LL NEVER GET MARRIED

"You understand, honey, I promised I would sacrifice to the Lord whatever came out of the house. We all know that little Lambkins has always been the first to greet us when we come home. But, I guess the Lord wants me to sacrifice you. Our Lord doesn't honor human sacrifice. Even Isaac was not sacrificed. God always provides a substitute. I could never do that anyway. But he does honor our lives given in sacrifice. I guess that means you'll have to devote your life in service to the Lord at the tabernacle."

A sob escaped his throat, and he wept aloud. "You'll never get married or have children."

"And she said unto her father, Let this thing be done for me: let me alone two months, that I may go up and down upon the mountains, and bewail my virginity, I and my fellows.

"And he said, Go. And he sent her away for two months: and she went with her companions, and bewailed her virginity upon the mountains." (Judges 11: 37-38)

Some Bible scholars inject into the discussion doubt of Jephthah's godly motives:

"Although the lapse of two months might be supposed to have afforded time for reflection, and a better sense of his duty, there is but too much reason to conclude that he was impelled to the fulfillment by the dictates of a pious but unenlightened conscience."[37]

Indeed, it surely seems that "too much reason," and not enough faith went into this explanation.

AND SHE KNEW NO MAN

But, what are the implications of the next section? Why did the Israelite nation make it a custom in Israel that their daughters lamented Jephthah's daughter four days every year? "And it came to pass at the end of two months, that she returned unto her father, who did with her according to his vow which he had vowed: and she knew no man. And it was a custom in Israel. That the daughters of Israel went yearly to lament the daughter of Jephthah the Gileadite four days in a year. (Judges 11: 34-40)

Why did she never mention the thought of dying, but spoke only of "bewailing her virginity" twice?[38] Why does the text attach two phrases together: "who did with her according to his vow which he had vowed:" and the phrase, "and she knew no man"? No doubt, the second phrase explains the first.

Zodiates poses this thought: "To say that his daughter spent her last two months of life up in the mountains with her friends rather than with her mourning father would have been peculiar. In addition to this, why is it that she bemoans her virginity rather than her short life? The phrase 'and she knew no man' would be meaningless if her life had been taken. It would seem more logical… that she was to be wholly given to the service of the Lord where she must continue her virginity."[39]

ACCORDING TO HIS VOW

The fulfillment of the vow is described somewhat ambiguously, "who did with her according to his vow which he had vowed…" (11: 39).

Henry M. Morris comments, "this does not say that he offered her as a burnt offering, merely that she "knew no man" throughout her life, in accord with her father's vow."[40]

J. Vernon McGee says, "What is meant is that he set her apart to perpetual virginity." And, "There is no indication that she was made a human sacrifice." [41]

The ultimate sacrifice for Jephthah was that his name would be forgotten and his posterity cut off. But, his name is NOT FORGOTTEN!

....

A NAME PRESERVED

Who can name any other man or woman of Jephthah's generation? This man, famous in his generation, gave up having his name remembered, but God preserved it forever!

Battalions of Bible scholars cannot seem to determine why Jephthah made such a vow. Ask what Jephthah did with his daughter to properly keep his vow. Few seem to know. Ask what is the main lesson learned in Sunday school about Jephthah— there is resounding silence.

IN THE BIBLE

Jephthah's story is a reminder of the words of the Lord Jesus Christ: "Heaven and earth shall pass away, but my words shall not pass away." (Matthew 24: 35)

Jephthah made a vow that required him, a Middle-eastern Jewish man, to remain childless. From that day on, he knew there would never be a "little Jephthah." Even though he had never had a son, perhaps he had retained the hope that someday his precious daughter would have a baby, a little grandson. They might name him Jephthah!

But now, because of his vow, he knew there would never be a son, a grandson, or a great-grandson. His name and his legacy would be forgotten. In fact, unlike other Bible names, his name still remains unselected when people choose names for children.

This is another way in which Jephthah appears to be a type of Christ. Isaiah prophetically asks concerning the Messiah, "who shall declare his generation? for he was cut off out of the land of the living…" (Isaiah 53: 8) Jesus, like Jephthah, had no progeny to preserve his name in history. Yet, no man in all of history is better or more widely known, quoted, revered and maligned, than the Lord Jesus Christ.

Like Jesus, Jephthah's burial place is uncertain (Judges 12:7). No Israeli tour guide can show you with 100% certainty the location of Jesus Christ's tomb, and even the town where Jephthah was buried is unknown.

A FORGOTTEN MAN

But, Jephthah is NOT forgotten! We are still reading, writing, and talking about him thirty-one centuries after his death. You are contemplating his story.

Drive through any town and read the names on the buildings: The Smith Building, Johnson Bank. Notice the names of streets: Wilson Street, Reagan Drive, Washington Boulevard. See the places of business: McDonald's, Wood Construction, Spark's Electric, Piper's Plumbing, Bud's Flowers, Flossie's Dental. Men are driven to leave their legacy—even if it lasts less than a hundred years.

But, here is a man who gave it all up to let God preserve his name, fully expecting it would be obliterated in a few decades. But God gave him a whole chapter in the only Book that will last throughout eternity!

WELCOME TO HEAVEN!

We have no record of Jephthah's obituary. Archaeologists have yet to discover his tombstone. Nobody knows how long he lived, or how long his daughter lived. When Old Testament saints died, they went to a place called Paradise. Jesus called it "Abraham's bosom." (Luke 16: 22) No human could enter Heaven until after the Lord Jesus Christ shed His precious blood on the cross, was buried, and rose again, defeating Satan, death, and hell.

When He arose from the dead, he ascended to Heaven as our High Priest, to present His blood on the Mercy Seat in the heavenly tabernacle (Hebrews 9: 11,14,23-26), making atonement for our sins.

Many Old Testament saints were seen in Jerusalem right after Jesus' resurrection (Matthew 27: 52-53). Then, we assume, their souls ascended to Heaven also. Since then, believers who die immediately ascend to Heaven (II Corinthians 5: 7).

Imagine Jephthah meeting Jesus in Heaven, "Welcome my friend. Come up here and sit beside Me. I've looked forward to visiting with you. I have something here I wanted you to see."

Boldly, Jephthah approaches the Throne. An angel assists him, as he makes himself comfortable, never taking his eyes off the Holy One.

THE BOOK

"Look in this Book, Jephthah. We've had this Book here 'forever… settled in Heaven.'" (Psalm 119:89)[42]

"Now, there's a part here that people didn't know about yet during your life on earth. It's a very important book about me, called Hebrews. Many of my people have claimed favorite verses from this book, especially the chapter that some preachers call 'The Faith Chapter' or 'The Hall of Faith.'"(Hebrews 11)

"This chapter explains what faith was. Of course, we don't need faith here in Heaven, because our faith has become sight! But, for the people who tried to understand and live by faith, we included some brief snippets of stories about some of the greatest people of faith. They are mostly people you already knew about on earth… like Abel, Enoch, Noah, Abraham, and Moses… By the way, that's him over there."

RAHAB THE HARLOT

Pointing at the page, the Lord Jesus gently continues, "I just wanted you to read some of them here: In verse 31 it tells about the amazing faith of the harlot Rahab—you remember about her, don't you?"

"Yes, Lord. I have always wondered about her. You see, my mother was a harlot, but I never knew much else about her. My wonderful stepmother and my humble daddy raised me."

"That's right, son, they loved you dearly," Jesus says. "Now listen to this: 'And what shall I more say? for the time would fail me to tell of Gedeon and of Barak, and of Samson, and of Jephthae… Who through faith subdued kingdoms, wrought righteousness…'"

Astounded, Judge Jephthah squints at the book. He turns to his Savior, Judge, and Deliverer, "You mean… You had my name preserved here for all time?"

"Yes, We did. And, I just want you to know, it's all because you took the step of faith to make your vow that day on the outskirts of Aroer, in Ammon, in obedience to the prompting of the Holy Spirit. We wanted the whole world to know that they can NEVER go wrong making a vow to the Lord from the pure motive of a heart of faith."

HE COULD HAVE MISSED IT

If Jephthah had not made the vow, he would have missed the opportunity to live out his life message. The central message of his life was: Make That Vow. You can't go wrong, if your motivation is pure, wanting to bring glory to God. There is eternal blessing in making holy vows to God, compelled by the Holy Spirit's prompting.

In fact, when God is leading, you cannot afford NOT to make the vow!

When David took refuge from King Saul in enemy territory, in Gath of Philistia, he feared that he would be "swallowed up." Fighting for his life every day, surrounded and oppressed, he wrote, "In God have I put my trust: I will not be afraid what man can do unto me. Thy vows are upon me O God: I will render praises unto thee. For thou hast delivered my soul from death: wilt thou not deliver my feet from falling that I may walk before God in the light of the living?" (Psalm 56: 11-13)

WHY DID DAVID VOW?

Is it possible that David thought of Jephthah's vow, when he spoke of his own?

David's spiritual mentor was the prophet Samuel, who wrote four books of the Bible, including Judges. No doubt Samuel, living at the end of the period of Judges, knew other legends and facts that could have been included, if the Holy Spirit had guided him to do so.

Perhaps Samuel and David had lengthy discussions about Jephthah and the wisdom of making vows to God. Maybe that is why David's writings and songs mention vows to God so frequently. Perhaps David's vows have something to do with the remark the Lord made about him in the New Testament, "I have found David the son of Jesse, a man after mine own heart, which shall fulfill all my will." (Acts 13: 22, Psalm 89:20, I Samuel 13: 14)

INSTEAD OF THE THORN... A NAME

Isaiah, speaking for the Lord, invites every one who thirsts to enter into a covenant vow, "Incline your ear, and come unto me: hear... and I will make an everlasting covenant with you, even the sure mercies of David." (Isaiah 55: 1,3) Many promises to those who enter such a covenant are listed in the following verses, but most notably, "Instead of the thorn shall come up the fir tree, and instead of the brier shall come up the myrtle tree: and it shall be to the Lord for a name, for an everlasting sign that shall not be cut off." (55: 13)

The dynamics of Jephthah's family had surely fallen into a state of thorns and briers. His father's adventure into prostitution had nearly destroyed all that was spiritual from the soil and fruitfulness of the family. Envy and strife prevailed in family relationships (James 3: 16), but Jephthah's vow restored the eternal perspective to the family, elevated his daughter to a lifetime of consecration, and established A NAME—an unassailable reputation for a man who had been known as "the son of an harlot." Even those who think Jephthah offered a human sacrifice must acknowledge that his vow to God forever changed his reputation!

What miraculous transformation of your name, reputation, and your life's productivity is awaiting the vow God has urged you to make?

JESUS CHRIST'S VOW

Jesus vowed to his own hurt, but he still kept His vow. No person who ever lived had integrity in such perfection as he did. And, no vow ever cost so much!

The words of his vow were prophesied by Isaiah centuries before Jesus spoke them, with absolutely unwavering determination and conviction, from human lips, "I was not rebellious, neither turned away back: I gave my back to the smiters, and my cheeks to them that plucked off the hair: I hid not my face from shame and spitting. For the Lord God will help me; therefore shall I not be confounded: therefore have I set my face like a flint, and I know that I shall not be ashamed." (Isa. 50: 5-7)

AND YOURS

What vow is God leading you to make? It could make all the difference in how your name will be remembered—especially when it really counts—in Eternity.

"The God of the mountain is still God in the valley."

—Tracy Dartt[4344]

....

A REAL VOW IN TODAY'S WORLD

Born in Minnesota, Tracy Dartt[45] moved to California as a teenager where he excelled in high school music and drama, and joined a teen chorale, The Christianaires. After he received Christ, he sang bass in The Stewards gospel quartet, and later with The Victors, who signed with Capitol Records and released "Brand New Feeling." The title song of the project was Tracy's first songwriting attempt.

Moving to Oklahoma, he joined the Weatherford Quartet, became a producer for Cam Records and helped launch Sound Factory Music Company. Returning to California, he and his wife, Sharon helped form another group, The Country Congregation. After that, he soloed, wrote and sang with Sharon on piano, for over a decade.

ONE FATEFUL NIGHT

One night, in 1988, he sang at a Baptist church in the mountain community of Auberry, California. They asked him to stay and be their pastor. He explained that he was a singer and songwriter. He said he would pray for them, but he had no experience as a pastor, and didn't want to be one. They were very insistent.

Representatives of the congregation finally got him to agree that he would pray about being their pastor. So, he prayed about it, reminding the Lord that his life goal was to be a songwriter, and pointing out that as a pastor, he would be so busy that he would not be able to write many songs.

But when he prayed, he felt strongly that the Lord wanted him to accept the call, and with some sadness, surrendered to do the will of God, abandoning his dream of writing songs that might bless many people.

GOD ON THE MOUNTAIN

That year, 1988, after surrendering his dream to answer God's call to the obscure mountain village church, The McKamey's live recording of his song, "God On The Mountain" leaped to the top of the Southern Gospel charts, and held the number one position on Singing News charts for 5 consecutive months. During that time, it drew more radio airplay points than any song in the history of Southern Gospel music up to that time.

MORE BLESSINGS

Tracy Dartt has written hundreds of gospel songs, recorded by the finest gospel musicians. But, "God On The Mountain" was nominated for a Dove award, and was recorded over 200 times by many artists including The McKameys, Lynda Randle, Jason Crabb, Jessy Dixon, Dixie Melody Boys, Jake Hess, John Starnes, The Weatherfords, and many more. The song has been recorded in at least eight different languages, featured on Bill Gaither's "Homecoming" videos, and sung frequently in Gaither's live "Homecoming" concerts.

After seven years at Auberry, a family gospel group, The Dartts was formed. Since 1995, they have toured and performed in concert from coast to coast.

When he vowed to abandon his dreams, like Abraham offering Isaac on Mount Moriah, Tracy Dartt entered a whole new arena of God's blessing. No longer attempting to manage his career and creativity, he accepted a position in a field for which he felt less than qualified. Almost immediately, God became his agent, guiding his song and his reputation as a songwriter to vistas he could not have anticipated.

Tracy Dartt humbly accepted God's assignment to a remote post where his name would be forgotten, but God rewarded him with a widely renowned reputation and a career of broad influence in churches among Christians, and in the field of Southern Gospel music.

"The thief walked out of prison a free man,
after he preached to the man he had robbed."

1 9

···

A BANK ROBBER'S VOW

When he was only nineteen, in the 1940's, Al Johnson[46] was convinced by an older man who had served time in prison that they could rob a bank and get away with it. They recruited another young accomplice, and targeted a bank in the small town of Hoyt, Kansas, north of Topeka.

Entering the bank, Al announced, "This is a hold up." The ex-convict brandished his weapon and ordered tellers to surrender the money. The seventeen-year-old bandit was assigned the job of retrieving money from the vault, but, afraid he might get locked inside, he balked.

With law enforcement coming, they fled. Al drove the getaway car. They ditched the car near the river, applied a substance to the soles of their shoes to confuse bloodhounds, and retreated to a shack on an island.

THE HIDEOUT

They waited several days, hiding in the cabin. Tension was high, because the loot only amounted to six hundred dollars. The older crook was angry, blaming the kid for their limited spoils, because the biggest prize still lay in the vault. Finally, he dispatched the novice to Topeka to scope out gossip about the robbery around town.

111

While the lad was gone, the ringleader proposed that he and Al divide the money and split, leaving the kid penniless. Johnson argued that they should give the kid his share. If they didn't, he thought the boy would likely squeal to the authorities.

UNEXPECTED NEWS

Suddenly, the kid returned from Topeka, bringing a newspaper with the latest news about the bank job. They read with interest.

Another gang of outlaws, recently escaped from prison, and driving a stolen car, attracted the police. A high-speed chase ensued and the crooks lost control, ending in a fatal crash. None of the gang survived.

Suspecting that the car thieves might also be the bank robbers, the police called the President and Vice President of the Hoyt Bank, who arrived at the accident scene and positively identified the dead men as the robbers.

The real robbers had a good laugh, congratulated themselves, divided the stolen money, and left the cabin, going their separate ways.

As he contemplated his good fortune at evading the law, Al decided that such high profile crime was not for him. He landed a job in a factory, and contented himself with petty theft of hubcaps, tires, and car parts.

A GIRL TOOK HIS EYE

About that time, he met a girl who took his eye. He asked for a date, but she turned it into an invitation to attend church. He accompanied her, and before long, realized that his only chance with Beth hinged upon his willingness to "get saved," which was constantly pressed upon the congregation by Pastor Brumme. Wanting to fit in and gain the approval of Beth and her family, Al went forward during the altar call, followed instructions, and "prayed the prayer." Like many others, Al thought he understood the gospel, and was soon baptized.

A MESSAGE IN THE MAIL

Before long, Al and Beth were married. But, his old crony met him after work one day and tried to talk him into pulling off another crime. Al refused, but only because he didn't want to take the chance of getting caught.

Then, one hot summer day, he decided to take a break from mowing the lawn. He retrieved the mail and glanced through it, sitting inside the house to cool off.

One envelope had no return address and no letter, but a gospel tract, "God's Simple Plan of Salvation," was enclosed. He began reading. The message emphasized the grace of God, and God's free offer of salvation. Suddenly, Al exclaimed to Beth, "This isn't right."

She sat down, and they read the tract together. She assured him that the message was exactly what the Bible teaches. Al realized he really had not been saved and an inner struggle began. He listened more intently to the pastor's messages, becoming increasingly convicted that he was a lost sinner, still in need of salvation. Heavy on his mind was the secret guilt of the bank robbery.

THE CONFESSION AND VOW

At last, he could bear it no more. With great emotion, he confessed the robbery to Beth, and explained that the guilt of sin had never lifted. He needed to be born again. After his prayer of repentance and faith, he vowed to the Lord that he would face the consequences, expecting certain prison time.

Together, they went to visit Pastor Brumme. Al confessed the crime privately in the pastor's study. The pastor affirmed that in order to obey God's Word, he would have to confess the crime to Law Enforcement.

THE VOW: CONFESSING ON THE RADIO

A unique plan was devised. The pastor called the Sheriff and explained that a crime would be confessed during the morning church service, which was broadcast over a network of radio stations. Al vowed to make full disclosure, and he did.

As he was arrested and taken from the church, photographers captured the scene, and reporters relayed the story to wire services. Newspapers and media outlets around the world, from Europe to Japan, ran the story and photo of the bank robber who confessed in church.

Meanwhile, Al was taken into custody, where he faced severe interrogation. The Sheriff was determined to get him to confess that they had made off with much more than the puny $600. Al provided information about his accomplices, and law enforcement began the search. Since the younger robber had enlisted in military service, he was not detained, but the old convict was soon apprehended.

Again, to no avail, interrogators pressured the old thief to admit that they had gotten much more money. There was no opportunity for collaboration between the robbers after Al's confession, so the lawmen were surprised that the robbers gave identical stories, including the mere $600 they had netted.

A BIGGER CRIME

Later, a more thorough investigation revealed that the chief officers of the Hoyt Bank had embezzled more than $30,000 over a period of time. This was why they had been so eager to identify the slain prison escapees as the Hoyt Bank robbers, hoping to see the case closed.

The Jackson County Attorney, preparing for the case, brought up a problem that Al, Beth, nor the pastor had anticipated. State law mandated a statute of limitations for prosecution of such crimes. Even though Al had already accepted the probability of prison, it seemed God had intervened in an amazing turn of events. The press reported it, and many citizens, including a Jewish merchant in Topeka, wrote to the pastor, expressing the viewpoint that God had honored Al's confession.

After indictments were brought against the bankers, the Sheriff remarked with sarcasm, "Johnson, I'll get you yet! You're the dumbest thief I ever met. Now, everybody knows what a crook you are, because you told it in church on the radio!"

Al replied, "Sheriff, I wouldn't change a thing. The world may think I'm a thief, but I know God has forgiven me, and I have peace in my heart. Better than that, I'm going to Heaven, because Jesus Christ paid for all my sins."

THE VOW FULFILLED

After he fulfilled his vow to tell the truth and suffer the consequences, Al Johnson discovered new freedom and joy. He and Beth really believed that he would face a prison sentence. They were amazed at the mercy and grace of God, as they relished the undeserved and unexpected deliverance they now enjoyed.

After they learned that the Statute of Limitations applied, Al entered into the life of the local church with renewed vigor.

Because of the close proximity of the church to state and federal prisons, a prison ministry team kept a regular schedule of preaching behind bars. Al was invited to join the prison ministry.

One Sunday afternoon, the prison team entered lockup, having assigned roles. Some had prepared special music. Another was the song leader. Al Johnson had agreed to preach. He told of his youthful thievery and the bank robbery. He recounted his guilt, Beth's testimony, the church youth group, the tract, and his surrender to Christ.

After the service ended, a man approached and said, "I am the man you held up." The former Hoyt Bank President, now incarcerated for embezzlement, thanked the one-time thief for his message. Al walked out a free man, and the banker remained behind bars.

Earlier, after Al was born again, he had gone to the banker's home with witnesses to pay back his part of the money taken in the robbery. The banker had refused his payment, advising, "Just keep this quiet. There's no need to let everyone know."

To be sure, not every vow has such a happy ending. And, Al Johnson's life has not been a picnic. Although he did not go to prison for the bank robbery, his family has been plagued with a variety of burdens, which has kept Al and Beth seeking the Lord's intervention in their lives. Satan continues his attack upon faithful servants of Christ.

IT ALL BEGAN WITH A VOW

In spite of setbacks, personal attacks, ridicule, embarrassment, and criticism, Al Johnson remained a faithful Christian, and served as an officer of his local church, holding various positions of responsibility for more than fifty years. He and Beth raised their family and built a lifelong business on the north side of Topeka, garnering the respect of the community, extending credit and assistance to hundreds of families, and supporting far-reaching missionary efforts around the world, youth workers, and evangelistic ministries inside and outside of prisons.

It all began with a vow to tell the truth with no rigged deals or under-the-table manipulations. Anticipating the pain of consequences, Al Johnson still told the truth. By God's grace, consequences were meliorated. But life on earth is still a battleground for every believer.

As it was for Jephthah, your integrity and faith is on trial when the Holy Spirit prompts. To vow or not to vow—that is the question.

"Many Christians names are so odious, that what they say or do is blemished… He is a dead man among the living that has a hateful name. It is a great mercy when our names outlive us; it is a great punishment when we outlive our names."

—William Jenkin[46]

....

YOUR VOW AND YOUR NAME

Vows were not simply an Old Testament custom. Paul and others made vows in the New Testament. Marriage vows are still headline news today.

Have you managed to remain neutral to the passion that burns within, a desire to fulfill God's Will, by merely avoiding the commitment of making a vow?

Could this be the moment that God has ordained for your vow? How long have you resisted the call of God to special service as a missionary, pastor or evangelist?

IT'S NOT TOO LATE

Samson's life was supposed to be all about living out his Nazarite vows—vows by which he was called to live before he was born. His story is mostly a tale of repeated incidents of his broken vows. (Judges 13-16) But, though his sins were many, and his end tragic, no one can deny the glorious answer to prayer that culminated in his final act!

Blind, chained, imprisoned, and ridiculed, no one would be shocked to learn that Samson hung himself in his prison cell, his vows shamefully forsaken, his purity defiled, and his reputation sullied. Instead, he rises to the highest ranks of Biblical heroes. Why? Because in a brief prayer, he snatched the prize from the teeth of defeat, and hurled it across the goalpost of victory!

Your children, grandchildren, cousins, and others are beset with addictions and attitudes that promise greater spiritual losses in their future. Jesus said, "This kind can come forth by nothing, but by prayer and fasting." (Mark 9: 29) Why don't you make a vow to God about your failure in intercessory prayer? How long will you continue to expect others to do your praying? When will you realize that your Saviour longs to commune with you?

You have struggled with financial issues. When will you come clean and acknowledge that your money problems are all rooted in your refusal to acknowledge God's ownership of all you possess? You sing, "This is my Father's World," and "He Owns the Cattle on a Thousand Hills," but He cannot expect a consistent ten percent of your income channeled into His work.

You really want to see your friends and loved ones come to Christ. There are times when you weep about their lost condition. But your commitment to regular times of witnessing and honing your soul-winning skills still takes a low position in your list of priorities.

THE POSSIBILITIES

Maybe like Jephthah, you've tasted the seamy side of life. The land of Tob, once inviting, turned out to resemble Dogpatch more than Utopia. Friends and family who reviled and hurt you now appear as welcome apparitions in your imaginary world of what-might-have-been.

THERE IS A GOD IN HEAVEN! His and His alone are the prerogatives of chance. What is prayer if not a presumption of the miraculous in the mud hole of despair?

It is your vow to make. Nobody else in the universe will ever have the opportunity you have right now. Your circumstances, your opposition, your character flaws, and the expectations of companions and foes are a recipe made for the miraculous.

Agonize as long as you wish, you cannot avoid the fact that the only alternative to the mundane and the mediocre is to cast your lot with the One Whose favor smiles upon the faith that risks it all.

Presidents and dictators plot and scheme to leave a legacy. Some individuals have been so desperate to have their name remembered that they even committed serial murder or genocide to have their names remembered, even in revulsion, for a few decades or centuries.

The Eternal Hall of Faith, like Hebrews chapter eleven, will surely feature names of those who risk everything, vowing to honor the Lord.

ENDNOTES

1. www.goodreads.com/quotes/tag/legacy

2. Steve Ragland and his wife, Margaret served on the author's staff from 1985-89.

3. http://www.goodreads.com/quotes/tag/legacy

4. M.C. Tenney (Ed.), Zondervan Pictorial Bible Dictionary. (Grand Rapids, MI: Zondervan, 1963), p. 742.

5. www.religionnews.com/2014/12/13/quote-day-supreme-court- justice-clarence-thomas/ Given in his speech at Palm Beach Atlantic University, Palm Beach, FL.

6. Reginald De Koven and Clement Clark. Oh Promise Me. (New York: G. Shirmer, Inc., 1889) Sheet music. This alternative verse was written by the author in 1968.

7. http://www.tennessee.gov/tsla/exhibits/myth/davycrockett.htm

8. Dictionary.com, definition 3

9. Wikipedia.com/WilliamCarey

10. E. Schuyler English (Ed.), The New Scofield Reference Bible. (New York: Oxford University Press, 1967) p. 303-304.

11. www.joniearecksontadastory.com

12. http://www.goodreads.com/quotes/tag/rejection

13. This is not the boy's actual name.

14. Wikipedia.com/Sarah Bush Lincoln

15. Op. Cit. (Tenney, 1963) p. 858

16. This is the Mizpeh located in Gilead, not Samuel's location near Bethel. There are several towns called Mizpeh (Mizpah) in the region.

17. Henry M. Morris, The Defender's Study Bible. (Iowa Falls, IA: World Bible Publishers, Inc., 1995) p. 299 notes the years served by each judge, plus years of oppression, yields 319 years from Numbers 21: 24- 26 to Jephthah's inauguration. By adding Jephthah's six years, the total is 325 years.

18. Ibid. p. 58.

19. F. Davidson (Ed.), The New Bible Commentary. (Grand Rapids,MI: Wm. B. Eerdmans Publishing Co., 1954), p. 250.

20. Frances E. Siewert (Ed.), The Amplified Bible. (Grand Rapids: Zondervan, 1965) p. 305.

21. Ibid.

22. The prohibition against adultery is the seventh commandment.

23. Op. Cit., (Tenney, 1963) p. 550.

24. Ibid.

25. Numbers 21:29.

26. Op. Cit., (Tenney, 1963) p. 153, 550.

27. Ibid.

28. Robert Jamieson, A.R. Fausset and David Brown, Commentary Practical & Explanatory of the Whole Bible. (London: Oliphants Ltd., 1961), p. 194-5.

29. John MacArthur, The MacArthur Study Bible. (Nashville: Word Publishing, 1997) p. 352.

30. Op. Cit. (Siewert, 1965).

31. Warren Baker, (Ed.), The Complete Word Study Old Testament. (Chattanooga: AMG Publishers, 1994) p. 678-9.

32. en.wikipedia.org/wiki/Jephthah

33. Josephus, Jewish Antiquities, trans., H. St. J. Thackeray and Ralph Marcus, Josephus V, Cambridge, MA. 1950, V. 8-10; cited in Thompson p. 107.

34. Op. Cit. (Baker, 1994), p. 678-9.

35. James Strong, A Concise Dictionary of the Hebrew Bible. (New York: Abingdon Press, 1963) p. 31, #1817

36. Ibid. (Strong, 1963) p. 45, #2897 & 2896—Tob means good, as in pleasure or prosperity.

37. Op. Cit., (Jamieson, Fausset and Brown, 1961).

38. Op. Cit., (Morris, 1995) p. 300, footnote: "Jephthah's daughter would have bewailed her coming death, not her virginity, if she was to be sacrificed… she bewailed… the fact that she would have to live her whole life without husband and children, performing service to the Lord, presumably… at the tabernacle."

39. Op. Cit., (Baker, 1994).

40. Op. Cit., (Morris, 1995).

41. J. Vernon McGee, Through the Bible, Vol. 2. (Nashville: Thomas Nelson Publishers, 1982), p. 71-2.

42. Op. Cit., (Morris, 1995). p. 1376, footnote on 10: 7: "The book of God had been written in heaven long before it was transmitted to men on earth… (Psalm 119:89, 139:16, I Peter 1: 18-20, Revelation 13: 8)." Hebrews 10: 7 quotes the Messianic prophecy in Psalm 40: 7-8, where, as in other passages (John 4: 34, 5:30, 6:38), the Lord affirms his purpose was "to do thy will, O God." In this respect, as in others, Jephthah is a type of Christ.

43. Tracy Dartt, *God on the Mountain*, Song # 162291, Manna Music, Inc., 1976, (Admin by ClearBox Rights, LLC), http://ca.search.ccli.com/

44. http://www.darttmusic.com/bio.html Some details of the story are based upon the author's memory of the testimony given by Tracy Dartt in concert.

45. Al and Beth Johnson are personal friends of the author.

46. William Jenkin, *Jenkin on JUDE*, Revised & Corrected by James Sherman (Beaver Falls, PA: Soli Deo Gloria Publications, 1652), p. 3.

ABOUT THE AUTHOR

....

C.T.L Spear is a storyteller and grandson of Oregon Trail pioneers. His published projects include Still a Kid! (Tate Publishing), Maranatha, the Miracle Camp (NE), Martin County Pictorial History (KY), Bedford County Family History (TN), and commemorative histories for the Fraternal Order of Police, and Sheriffs in Denver, Nashville, Fort Worth, and St. Paul (Turner Publishing Company).

Spear and his wife, Sharen, toured in Rally-concerts and youth outreach from Denver. He founded KCEB-FM radio, and was a prison Chaplain for five years. Their children and grandchildren live in Canada, Virginia, and Texas.

Hourglass Ministries: www.hourglassministries.com
www.facebook.com/CT Spear
www.facebook.com/CTL Spear
Dittydad@Twitter.com
Book site: www.stillakid.com
C.T.'s blog: http://dangerstoilsandsnares.com